OUT OF TH
INTO

THE NINE-YEAR CHANGE
THROUGH THE STORIES OF
THE THIRD GRADE CURRICULUM

OUT OF THE GARDEN AND INTO THE DESERT:
THE NINE-YEAR CHANGE THROUGH THE STORIES OF THE THIRD
GRADE CURRICULUM

All rights reserved.

Copyright © 2015 by Neal & Jennifer Kennerk
Interior art by Neal Kennerk

This book is protected under the copyright laws of the United States of America. Thank you for not reproducing, scanning, or distributing any part of it without the permission of the author.

First Printing: March 2015

First Edition: March 2015

For Arwen & Harper

TABLE OF CONTENTS

INTRODUCTION

The Nine-Year Old.. 7
The Lunar Nodes and the Breathing Process of the
Earth... 9
The Four-Fold Human Being... 12

1. CONSCIOUSNESS AND THE ARCHETYPES

The Stream of Change - An Overarching
Image.. 15
Use of the Old Testament.. 20
Symbols of Authority in Genesis... 28
Symbols of Experience & Ego in Genesis........................... 32

2. THE GARDEN AND THE FORBIDDEN FRUIT

The Garden of Eden... 39
The Forbidden Fruit... 42

3. OUT OF THE GARDEN AND INTO THE DESERT

Adam & Eve - Beginning the Journey................................. 51
Death & Sorrow - a New Understanding............................. 56
Cain & Abel - Light and Shadow... 62

The Two Selves - Shadow and Light.................................... 65
Tubal Cain - Transformation & Home Life...................... 67
Noah & the Flood - Self-Sufficiency.................................... 71
The Tower of Babel - Unabashed Arrogance.................... 75

4. THE PROMISED LAND

God's Covenant with Abram - Anticipating the Future.. 81
The Future Realized... 86
Abram & Lot - Out With the Old & In With the New....... 91
Sodom & Gomorrah - Questioning Authority.................. 93
A New Name - Individuation.. 96
The Sacrifice of Isaac - Letting Go..................................... 99
Isaac & the Ram - Sorting Through the Past.................. 101
Digging Wells - Preserving the Past................................. 105
Jacob & Esau... 108
Birthright & the Stream... 111
Wresting in the Darkness with a Vision of the Light... 116
Joseph - the First Born Son of Israel & Rachel............... 123
Individuation, Dreams, Exclusion, & Self-Authority....... 129

5. JOB, MOSES, & GOD - A CONCLUSION

Job & the Purpose of Suffering... 142
Moses Sees the Light of Self... 150

Bibliography... 161

INTRODUCTION

"Between the ninth and tenth years,....a child gradually awakens to the difference between self and the surrounding world. Only then does a child become aware of being a separate I."
Rudolf Steiner, *The Child's Changing Consciousness* lecture 5

The Nine-Year Old

Nothing can be more difficult than trying to parent or teach a child who is going through the nine-year change. They are moody, secretive, assertive and volatile. One minute they are cuddling with you on the couch, and the next they are storming off to their room and slamming the door on the way, while we are left wondering 'what happened?'

Young children live in a world free from hardship, and are intimately connected with their environment. They see goodness in everything and have explicit trust in the adults who care for them. It is a blissful state of unconsciousness. When children turn nine, this trusting, unconscious relationship with the world begins to change.

Children at this age experience an inner crisis, where they begin to question all the truths they have blindly held before. They wonder about their purpose in the world, and about the purpose of the world itself. They wonder whether or not the adults in their lives really know everything about right and wrong, or good and evil. Not surprisingly, the array of emotions and behaviors displayed are intense and varied. Before the age of nine, your child lives in a garden of paradise and then swiftly, without warning, they fall.

In a series of lectures published as *The Child's Changing Consciousness*[1], Steiner talks about the child as she begins to separate from the world around her, becoming aware for the first time that she is an individual. No one would argue that this is a monumental feat, but why is this happening?

---

[1] Steiner, Rudolf *The Child's Changing Consciousness* (New York: Anthroposophical Press, 1988), lecture 5

The Lunar Nodes and the Breathing Process of the Earth

In lecture four, in a series entitled *Man: Hieroglyph of the Universe*[2], Steiner explains how the macrocosmic breathing process in the heavens connects to the microcosmic breathing process of the earth, and how this course is run in a rhythmic cycle every 18.6 years. This is expressed in the *ascending* lunar nodes, and has a direct impact on human biography, for every 18 years, 7 months, and 9 days the moon is in the exact same place on the earth's ecliptic as it was on the day we were born. Steiner said that these nights of our lives are some of the most significant that we will ever experience. He tells us that not only are these particular nights of great importance, but the periods of time directly before and after. These points in time ask us to give up something of great importance that no longer serves the maturation process of our souls. At each of these junctures, the soul experiences a rebirth into a new chapter of life.

---

[2] Steiner, Rudolf *Man: Hierglyph of the Universe* (Bn 201, GA 201) Lecture four

The first lunar node is characterized by breaking away from one's family. The individual is now ready for a new level of autonomy and needs to set off, away from what the individual has known before.

The second lunar node tasks us with breaking away from social constructs that hinder the pre-birth impulse. This is a time where we often embark on a new career, or sever ties with friends or peers that no longer serve to further our karma. Each node thereafter has a similar theme – an actual severance with an experience in the physical world.

The *descending* lunar nodes also have their impact. These occur at the halfway points between the ascending lunar nodes. These nodes are also an experience of rebirth and breaking away, but with the descending nodes, the severance happens *internally*. During these phases of life, the soul is working on aspects of itself that have a more archetypal quality. Soul development at this time will focus on shedding internal beliefs that will inhibit further soul development. We also awaken to new levels of consciousness that allow us to adopt new paradigms and perspectives that will aid in future development of the soul. If we do some math, we will see that the first descending node occurs at nine and one third years. This is the nine-year change.

The Four-Fold Human Being

The occurrence of the nine-year change is brought on by the descending lunar node, which causes the soul to leave things behind that are no longer needed and then adopting more appropriate belief structures that will advance soul development. To put it more simply, childhood is lost and ego-consciousness is born.

This understanding of ego-consciousness is derived from the anthroposophical teachings of Rudolf Steiner. An understanding of anthroposophy and spiritual science as it pertains to child and human development will be helpful while reading this book, but are not essential. However, since the nine-year change is sponsored by a deeper penetration of the ego, this book does refer to "ego" and "ego-consciousness" regularly. In order to have an understanding of these concepts, the following explanation of Steiner's four-fold human being is offered:

The Physical Body - The physical body is that part of us that is visible. It is our flesh and bones. It is related to the mineral world, and is subject the same laws of the physical, mineral world. The physical body is lifeless, and when not imbued with a life force, will wither and die away.

The Etheric Body – The etheric body is the life force that holds up the physical body. It is that aspect of life that we share with the plant world. All plants, animals, and humans have an etheric body.

The Astral Body – The astral body is the soul of the human being. This is where consciousness lives. It is the source of feeling, impulse, and instinct. The astral body is related to the animal world, and this element is shared with the animal kingdom.

The Ego Body – The ego body is the divine element of the human being, and is unique to the human being. It is the eternal aspect of ourselves that is carried throughout time and incarnations. The ego works on, and penetrates the other parts of the four-fold human being.

Housekeeping Note:

Throughout this book, "ego" will refer to the Ego-Body element of the four-fold human being, "ego-consciousness" will refer to an awareness of this ego element, and "Self" will refer to an inner manifestation of the ego and/or ego consciousness.

1. CONSCIOUSNESS & THE ARCHETYPES

*"Rudolf [Steiner] once spoke of a stream that seeped away
in one place
and then welled up again somewhere else;
he compared certain soul-processes in human beings
with this phenomenon in nature.
Such processes can vanish into the inner depths of the
human being,
to emerge again at a later time in a changed form."*
Hermann Koepke Encountering the Self

The Stream of Change – An Overarching Image

Across the landscape there flows a stream. It dances and laughs as it trips across the rocks. Suddenly, and without warning, it disappears from sight. We may be fooled into thinking that the waters have vanished, but they are still flowing forcefully below the surface. The rushing stream has fallen into a hidden, underground channel. These waters are working their way deep into the earth, finding the depths of the cavernous passages before they rise again to the earth's surface. The stream re-emerges fortified, purified, renewed -

and we all want to take a drink. We understand that something has happened to this water, although what it is, we cannot say. All we know is that the water has been transformed, and that it is all the better for it.

Rudolf Steiner used the image of this stream that suddenly dives into the earth, resurfacing in another time and place to describe what is happening in the soul-life of the child during the nine-year change. It is a powerful image with many indications. The child, like the stream, is going along much the same way he always has when suddenly, the child you thought you knew so well has completely disappeared. Something has changed for him and the innocence he has enjoyed thus far is disappearing at a rapid pace. Without warning, and without the knowledge that it was going to happen, he falls.

What happens then is difficult to see, but we must trust that it is work that needs to be done. This work is not easy – and the behavior that is often seen during this time reflects that. The child's life course takes a deep and immediate plunge beneath the surface as he faces a land of darkness and shadow. This stream will continue on its downward trajectory, and these shadows will continue to be the focus for our children for some time. Thankfully, there is light at their backs as they make this descent, and they are reminded of it whenever they turn around. As much as they would like to return, they know they cannot, and instead move further and further away. For a time, they are so deep below the ground that there is no light at all. This is the worst part for the children and is when their behavior will be the most extreme. Children must confront, cognize, and work with the shadow before they can forge on and see the light ahead. Hopefully, the child presses on quickly, and moves forward at a good pace. Eventually, the stream will rise back toward the surface, and they can once again live in a place filled with light. However, this is not the same light of childhood they had known before. Instead, they see the light of adulthood streaming in from the opening that will return them to the surface.

While "underground" during this time of development there are universal, archetypal truths that all children are working on. Each child must make the initial "fall", learn to cope with their new surroundings, fend for themselves, learn to hear their inner voice, wrestle with their shadow side, find redemption, and return to the surface. While it is important at every stage of development, it is especially crucial during the nine-year change that children are met with the same archetypal images from the outside, that they are experiencing on the inside. In this way, the soul is being worked harmoniously from within and from without, nourishing the the soul in it's development.

Rudolf Steiner suggested that the images of the Old Testament offer the child the correct external imprint to match the internal one during this time, and these are the traditional stories of the Waldorf third grade curriculum. The following chapters of this book are an attempt to tie the stories of the Old Testament to the specific work of the soul during the nine-year change.

It can be seen as a journey, beginning with "the fall" of Adam and Eve, which is the moment our aforementioned "stream" takes it's plunge. The proceeding stories of the Old Testament represent the work of the child while under the earths surface. They represent all the previously mentioned archetypal elements that each child is tasked with until finally, they reach the surface again.

Use of the Old Testament

In Waldorf schools the world over, children in the third grade hear the stories of the Old Testament. These stories reflect an inner journey happening in the soul life of the child. This is the beauty of Waldorf education; the curriculum uses archetypes to mirror the inner soul development. This is the case in each year, from the fairytales of first grade to World history in eighth grade. These images imprint divine knowledge from the outside, just as the soul is having the same experience inwardly. This archetypical matching imbues the academic curriculum with something that is alive and eternal so that the child can take the curriculum in on a very deep level.

Just as the archetypes bring the academic information alive for the child, the archetypes can enliven our understanding of the child's soul development. To enhance our knowledge of the nine-year change, we can examine the archetypes in the stories of Genesis, interweaving them with the experience of this pivotal moment in human development. The nine-year change marks a shift from the unconscious state of childhood, in which the child and the surrounding world are perceived as one, to an awakening where individuality is realized.

The first descending lunar node marks the death of childhood and the birth of the Self. It is a breaking away from childhood innocence and a coming to terms with the (sometimes harsh) realities of the world. During early childhood, Steiner informed us that children must be taught through goodness because children naturally believe that the world is a good place. The nine-year change marks a paradigm shift away from this intrinsic belief. Not only must they face the reality that the world is capable of shadow, but that they themselves carry the capacity for shadow. To meet this tumultuous time in the child's life, the Waldorf third grade curriculum uses the stories of the Old Testament to mirror this internal struggle.

There is a direct correlation between the stories of the beginnings of the Hebrew peoples, and the beginnings of ego-consciousness for the child during this intense time of development.

The archetypes in Genesis from the Fall of Adam and Eve, to the rise of Joseph, are inspiringly deep and can illuminate the experience of the child so that as adults, we may empathize and guide them through this time of change. It is no coincidence that Steiner suggested the stories of the Old Testament for the third grade curriculum. These stories are archetypal, and a near perfect image of the trials and tribulations that are occurring within the soul life of the child during this time. At each stage of development, Waldorf curriculum brings the correct archetypes to the child which reflect the archetypal images they are experiencing internally. In this way, proper imprinting can take place and the academic curriculum will be received on a much deeper level.

It is important to understand that the stories of the Old Testament are not presented as either fact, or religious doctrine. Some Waldorf teachers present these stories as

Hebrew Mythology. They are presented in the same manner as the fairytales of first grade, the stories of saints and fables in second grade, or 4th grade Norse Myths. While the teacher always presents the story with reverence, it stems from a reverence of the archetype.

Archetypes are experiences and processes that all human beings recognize and hold in common: birth, growth, death, love, loss, revenge, struggle, duality, transformation, exclusion, vision, etc. They represent the themes of humanity. The power the archetypes hold is plain to see, but can be difficult to explain. They evoke feelings deep within us, and can guide us through each stage of soul development. Archetypes are representations of the behaviors of the human soul that are eternally repeated. Archetypes are the foundation of all stories - fiction or nonfiction. They permeate literature, life, music, color—wherever experience can be found. Because they resonate throughout human experience and cognition, they possess a certain power to guide us through the possibilities and probabilities of the infinite paths flowing outward from every experience. Archetypes are developmental pictures of human experience and the true lessons of life. The archetypes found within the Old Testament can offer us insight into the soul development of the child during the nine-year change, just as they gave meaning to our ancestors throughout struggles of adversity, giving them the strength and knowledge to make it through life's ups and downs.

The nine-year change can be quite a stressful time for both the child and parents. The child has never before experienced the shadow of humanity as they do now. This new understanding will cause them to question everything they once knew and have previously believed, including the trusted adults in their life. This questioning is essential if the child is to find their own inner voice, but it can lead to unwanted and defiant behavior. If parents and teachers are to help guide the child through this time in a productive way, they must be able to see this transition objectively.

The ability to understand the child's behavior through archetypal representation allows the adults in the child's life to observe and guide them objectively. Objective knowledge provides a 'distancing' between ourselves and our own reactions to the child's behavior. This 'distancing' is essential for maintaining a presence of authority so that we, as adults, may meet the child with a loving, but firm presence. We model strength of ego for the child—showing the child what the ego can be. Since parents and teachers love their children, they naturally have a subjective bond that can lend itself to reaction. It is easy to allow our own internal reactions to guide our interaction with our children. When our children begin to push us away, we naturally feel a great deal of personal rejection. Instead of seeing this rejection as a natural stage of soul development that the child must pass through, we may react as erratically as the child! Objective observation must be brought consciously to strengthen our own ego presence, which in turn will naturally provide the appropriate boundaries and guidance the child is seeking.

As we tie the images found in the Old Testament together with the internal struggle of the nine-year old, it is essential to establish and explain a few concepts and archetypal images in order to move more efficiently through the interweaving ideas contained within the body of this book. While exploring such things, we must keep in mind that the child is experiencing an emergence of ego-consciousness, which is forcing a separation between the child and the outer world. As Hermann Koepke states in *Encountering the Self*:

> It is the ego being of the child that is trying to enter. That is one thing that is too little noticed and unfortunately far too little supported. The other is that the beautiful childhood-world has to be left behind; it sinks out of sight. Fear then arises in the child.[3]

This new consciousness is the inspiration for new behaviors, and the behaviors are how the child processes fears and

---

[3]Koepke, Hermann *Encountering the Self* (New York: Anthroposophical Press, 1989), 21

uncertainties. Behaviors should be observed as language, for they are how the child communicates their experience.

Proactively understanding the nine-year change can lend a greater possibility for objectivity in observation and a healthy response to intense behaviors—passive or aggressive. Koepke stated that the child's ego is awakening. This awakening can lead to a capacity for quiet wonder, but it can also lead to a tendency to criticize. The child needs to feel loved and feel safe in the fact that there is still truth and beauty within them and within the world. We must give them stability, so that they can come to consciousness in a manner that allows them to build the ego with autonomy of feeling and individuality in action.

Symbols of Authority in Genesis

> *"....with his dawning sense of ego the child takes his first step onto the earth, and human teachers take over from divine powers the task of guiding him to manhood."*
> A. C. Harwood, The Recovery of Man in Childhood

Even with our knowledge of the child's experience and the provision of practical algorithms and pictorial archetypes, the child will still resist ego-consciousness and its formation. The child needs an authority that can handle their new situation. The loss of Paradise will undoubtedly be the source for new kinds of behaviors. The child's behavior intensifies in relation to several new realities of which they are becoming aware—feeling separate from the world, loss of childhood, etc. They feel alien and alone in a world they no longer recognize—a perceptual shift has taken place. They need a guiding voice.

In Genesis, this internal guide is represented by the voice of God, while the world is represented by the harsh desert. In order to survive this caustic landscape the child needs to feel they have their own inner authority, but it requires that as adults, we act as a model for that authority. The child can then begin to hear their *own* inner guiding voice. The child will often reflect the tendencies and characteristics of the adults around them. If adults model their own strong ego and deep knowledge of Self, then the child will correlate this with the guiding voice of God-the great mentor. Of course we are speaking metaphorically, but as you can see, these images are archetypal, explaining their use throughout time. We are using these images because of these archetypal qualities and for their correlation to humanity.

Adults can also be likened to the land of Egypt and Pharaoh, which were authorities and mentors for the Hebrews in the world of Genesis. The land of Egypt had already established itself within the world in so many ways - much like the adult. Egypt represents the adult's knowledge of self-sustainability, practical arts, developed belief structures, structured governance, and individuality as a civilization—some of the things that the Hebrew people had yet to achieve. The Pharaoh is also a symbol of the adult's authoritative presence in the stories of Abram and Joseph.

As God archetypes, adults must recognize that the child is acting out of a new and intense experience of reality. Realizing this can help us to avoid taking their extreme behaviors personally, and possibly losing their trust while modeling an impulsive or reactionary ego. We need to look to the God of Genesis for our inspiration. God creates Adam and Eve and cares for them. He has the ability to punish them for breaking his commandments and eventually sends them out into the world alone, trusting that they have learned what is needed to survive. This is a very similar picture to the task of parents. We create our children, nurture them, provide appropriate discipline and eventually send them out as free adults, hoping we have given them the knowledge and tools needed to succeed on their own.

We must model our own strength of ego so that children can gain a sense of how to do this for themselves.

God allows his children to stumble and fall with the firmness of authority and the love of a parent, while guiding them to the land of promise. In order to effectively parent during the nine-year change, there must be sympathy for the child, for this is truly an intense time. However, it is important not to be overly sympathetic. This is a time for children to test limits and boundaries, and to try on more adult behavior. It is important to realize this and not be reactionary. If we understand that intense and erratic behaviors are actually a part of development, then we are less prone to react harshly —the child has enough harshness in their new world. If guided in a loving, but firm way, the child will embrace her parent or teacher as a strong ego presence who is worthy of following. They will see the creative forces at work in their teachers and parents—as well as the fruits of this work. It can be much more effective to parent by example, than instruction. Our behavior works in the subconsciousness of the child at a time when overt statements and requests will surely be questioned!

Symbols of Experience and Ego in Genesis

Consciousness is the root of all struggles. Without consciousness, problems do not exist, for there is no ego center through which to conceptualize and make judgments. A struggle is only a struggle because of an opposition created by a separation from the whole—the distinction between the Self and the world. Adam and Eve were not aware of so many things--their own nakedness for example. But, with the eating of the forbidden fruit - with their awakened self-consciousness, the world becomes a different place. They are now naked and beginning to feel the cold and the heat, the toil and the strife, and all of the realities of existence that were not perceived before eating the forbidden fruit. Struggles now exist in the tension between the longing for childhood and the difficult adaptation to the path of adulthood.

The child now begins to compare and contrast the oneness experienced in childhood to the separation experienced through the dawning of ego-consciousness. The child feels so many new feelings about this abrupt change which marks the beginning of the rest of their life. They will instinctually resist this change, and they must to a certain degree. They must deal with their struggles and own them in order to master them and build a strong foundation upon which the ego will expand. They will make desperate dashes for the gates of Eden and attempt, in various ways, to re-enter the paradise of light. But, alas, there is no return, and the child must face the harsh desert and learn to listen to the voice of the Self.

The inevitable struggles of the nine-year change are the archetypes of human experience. As humans, we experience them throughout our lives, but as we gain knowledge of them through experience and understanding, they become less and less of a struggle. However, they seem monstrous as the nine-year old faces them for the first time. If you've ever returned to an environment that you haven't been to since you were a child, you will notice how utterly tiny everything has become, yet you know that it is you that has gotten bigger. As the ego grows exponentially with self-awareness, the perception of the world and it's struggles become manageable.

The main characters of each story of the Old Testament--from Adam and Eve to Joseph—represent the child's evolving ego-consciousness. They are the symbols for ego. The ego becomes conscious of several archetypal realities such as death, sorrow, duality, purification, arrogance, faith, sacrifice, struggle, vision, individuation, self-knowledge, and forgiveness. These are but a few of the archetypes of human experience waiting to be perceived by the emerging ego. But make no mistake - it requires an ever-growing ego-consciousness to steadily expand awareness so the child may begin to examine Self in relation to the now separate world. The experience of the child separates and opens a conscious dialogue between the Self and the world, and this dialogue is mediated by the ego - as each character in the Old Testament is the medium between the voice of God and their experiential quest into the desert.

The plot of each story, the imagery of changing landscapes as the ego wanders further, and the struggles to live into the harsh desert world represent the archetypes of human experience that the nine-year old is awakened to with the first glints of ego-consciousness. These are the archetypes that serve to forge the ego, to give it foundation and presence in the world, and to make it present within the child. The archetypes are offered through stories and pictoral lessons, as well as through firsthand experiences.

For the nine-year old, practical archetypal experiences such as farming and house building can offer the a powerful example of nourishing and protecting the Self , not only in a physical manner, but also for nourishing and protecting the metaphysical aspects of the human spirit. The archetypes, or algorithms of farming (growing, tending, nourishing) and building (constructing, putting together, protecting), show the nine-year old child how we as humans can provide--for our body, our feelings, and our thinking—a form to life through which we can nourish ourselves, protect ourselves, and assert our will self-sufficiently. The building of structures reflects the building of the physical body in which the ego is beginning to inhabit, and gardening reflects the process of self cultivation and nourishment. This is why these activities are woven into the yearly rhythm of the third-grade school year.

The child needs this practical application of self-reliance, for the *change* has separated them from the garden where nourishment and protection are provided without effort. They are thrust into the harsh desert of consciousness in which they can feel alone and alien. This practical work shows them that they have the tools to make their way in this new world, and overcome these new-found fears. As parents and teachers, we should neither abandon them nor coddle them, for we need to give a type of guidance that speaks to the child and illuminates how they can individually walk the path they are intended to.

The Hebrew people were a wandering people that searched for the land that is promised by God — the child is an ego wandering through a harsh new land in search of a place where inner and outer worlds begin to forge a conscious relationship with one another. They are learning about the world in a deeper way, in order to find individuality, autonomy, goodness, and beauty.

The Hebrew people ventured out into the land where they would live with the God that guides them. They established individuality by listening to their God and working with the land. The better they got at hearing God, the more they were blessed by the land, and the better they got at tending the land, the easier it became to adapt to new experiences. The same for the child – they have entered an unfamiliar land and must now learn to navigate it.

2. THE GARDEN & THE FORBIDDEN FRUIT

"For children, everything is one, and they are also one with their surroundings."
Rudolf Steiner, *The Kingdom of Childhood*

The Garden of Eden

Life in the garden is blissful for Adam and Eve. The paradise of Eden is an idyllic place where the spiritual fruit of God's creation hangs from the trees and requires no toil or strife in order for it to flourish. Hopefully, childhood is also a blissful time, where the child knows little about the worry and work of the adults that provide the sustenance that they receive, whether it is physical or spiritual nourishment. The child is unconscious of so much and that is what makes childhood similar to the Garden of Eden. Adam and Eve possess a feeling of safety - in fact, they feel so safe that they move about the garden unclothed and unaware of nakedness —like the young child, they are completely exposed.

Before the fall from Eden, the child has not yet made any serious attempt to intellectually separate themselves from the peaceful hum of the world around them. The unconsciousness of Self, as separate from the world provides a wonderment, utopia, and openness that facilitates transcendence from the sufferings of self-consciousness. Ideally, the child is without judgment, lasting emotional pain, existential angst, or abstract conceptualization of the world. We adults must be sensitive to this, as Steiner writes in *The Kingdom of Childhood*:

> Children, especially at the age between the change of teeth and puberty, are most sensitive as to whether teachers are governed by imagination or intellect. The intellect has a destructive and crippling effect on children; imagination gives children life and impulse.[4]

This imaginative approach is not impulsiveness, but the creative impulse of the human being. This impulse honors their solipsism within the unconsciousness of childhood—within the fantastical world of pure experience.

---

[4] Steiner, Rudolf *The Kingdom of Childhood* (New York: Anthroposophical Press, 1995), 33

Now, as you have been reading, you may have thought to yourself that your child exhibits all sorts of adult behavior – and this may indeed the case! The child may exhibit adult impulses, but only because they imitate the behaviors of the adults around them. They exhibit the behavior, but not the depth of consciousness. We must not assume that they are intellectually thinking - the child merely imitates the adults in their life. They are unconscious to such thought and must remain so, for it would rob them of the pure experience of childhood and the essential growth arising from such experience. It is through adults that the child begins to imitate and understand the simple rules of the garden.

The Forbidden Fruit

> *"It is the sacrifice of the merely natural man, of the unconscious, ingenious being whose tragic career began with the eating of the apple in Paradise. So, the child has eaten the 'forbidden fruit' and is coming to the same realizations that Adam and Eve faced. It is the beginning of the rest of their lives. The biblical fall of man presents the dawn of consciousness as a curse. And as a matter of fact it is in this light that we first look upon every problem that forces us to greater consciousness and separates us...from the paradise of unconscious childhood."*
> Carl Jung, The Portable Jung

God gave Adam and Eve one simple rule for life within Eden - do not eat fruit from the tree in the center of the garden. God tells them not to eat from the tree of knowledge. If they do they will be doomed to die. For quite some time, Adam and Eve comply with this request, but one day their curiosity cannot be stayed any longer. This same scenario in happening inwardly for your child. The "fruit" is intellectual knowledge. Your young child will have no interest in this fruit for many years, however they too will eventually become just as curious as Adam and Eve, and eventually, cannot control themselves any longer and will take a bite. Thankfully, their consequence will not be death—it will be the end of unconscious childhood. For now the child is unaware of the realities and concepts concerning mortality, struggle, feeling alone and separate, or their future encounter with their ego.

It is inevitable that one day, the child can stay their curiosity no more, and they take a bite of the forbidden fruit. While this is indeed inevitable, it is important to ensure that children do this on their own time. Many teachers and parents unknowingly serve this fruit up freely to children too early, without realizing the impact. Children, out of curiosity, often ask for this fruit before they are truly ready, but we should try and refrain from giving it to them. When the young child asks the question "why is the sky blue?", the last thing they need is a detailed explanation of atmosphere, reflection, refraction and the like. This is dead and hardening information that does nothing to nourish the soul development of the child. Since they do not have the intellectual capacity (as smart they undoubtably are) to fully understand abstract concepts, they come to mistrust their own powers of observation. The best answer, as long as it will satisfy, is "I wonder". This answer will be enough for many years. When "I wonder" is no longer enough, you can move to "what do you think?". These open ended answers teach young children to trust that what they see and believe is right - and this is what they need - whether it is actually correct or not. Scientific explanations should come after the child has the capacity to fully understand and engage with the information. Just because they can recite memorized facts, does not mean that they have a working relationship with the concepts.

We want children to trust their own powers of observation. This builds self-trust, which is crucial for maintaining confidence during the nine-year change and beyond. A common observation of the young child comes as they gaze at the setting sun. "The sun goes around the earth", they say. If you correct this before the appropriate time, you do nothing but tell them that they cannot trust what they see, creating self-doubt. "I see that too" is a much more encouraging response that does not provide incorrect information. That is exactly what you see as you look to the sky, and you should be happy your child is paying attention to her surroundings. The technical information can wait until after the ninth or tenth year, when the child is capable of understanding the concepts - after they have taken a bite of the apple.

Often, parents ask what harm it does if the children learn facts and figures too early. The answer is none and a lot. Of course children will pick things up here and there, especially if they have older siblings in the house. Not only is this inevitable, but this is the karmic path the child has put herself on. The young child may be quite proud that she is able to rattle off facts that her older brother or sister has brought home, and this is fine. What is not fine is for the parents to give too much attention to it. If a kindergarten child shows an interest in flowers, and happens to pick up a fact or two about them, parents get very excited about this and start to explain all sorts of scientific information about flowers and their life cycles and such. This is not what feeds a connection between the child and a flower. This type of scientific information - if given too early - can actually create a barrier between the child and the very thing the parent is trying to endear her to.

In addition to having a hardening effect on the soul, this kind of scientific information can also separate the child from her connection to the cosmos. It is a great gift that young children are able to maintain this connection with the spiritual world. This connection helps the child in all she does, from the growing of the physical body and all it's organs, to maintaining a healthy life sense until she is able to maintain it herself. When children are forced to 'wake up' too early, this spiritual connection begins to fade, and the child is responsible for things they are not yet ready for. This can lead to sickness, anxiety, or attention difficulties. So often, there are children in the kindergarten that are thin, pale, and nervous; they do not look healthy. If you have a chat with these children, very often you will find that they are quite bright and full of information. They know many things about many things, but they have trouble lifting their arms over their heads! This is a child who thought that the apple looked pretty good to eat, and the adults in her life began to hand out slices. Let your child pick the apple herself and decide the rate at which she will eat it.

It is the apple that represents the capacity for more abstract thinking. The fruit comes from a tree of knowledge - a knowledge of good and evil, of light and shadow. This fruit wakes them up and gives them a new-found consciousness. The expression "you are what you eat", applies nicely in this situation for the child is now taking on the aspects of the fruit, both of the light, and the shadow. Children become very concerned with the opposition of good and evil at this time.

Each child will digest this fruit differently. There are as many varying reactions to be had from eating this fruit as there are from eating wheat, dairy, or spices. Some take one bite and then go on to devour the entire thing. Some slowly nibble over the course of many months. Some love fruit, and some do not. Some children are more than ready to wake up, and some would prefer to sleep as long as they are allowed. The child must be able to make their own way, at their own pace, through their own awakening.

Remember, that Adam and Eve are not expelled from the garden the instant they eat the fruit. It is the gradual absorption of the fruit that brings the dawning realization of their nakedness. The ego gradually descends and nourishes the growth of consciousness. God comes to them and they hide because of their new-found consciousness. This is their first lesson in good and evil, and it is only after a lengthy foreshadowing of life to come, that God finally escorts them to the gates. The ego emerges as a conscious center, standing between the world and the Self—separating and pulling the Self into the body and out of the environment. The same is true for children. They do not instantly "wake up" with their first bite — they slowly come into consciousness the more they absorb. But, it is with this first bite that they begin life outside the garden, and into the desert.

This is a necessary stage of development that causes the child to individuate. Until they begin eating the apple, they are still very much apart of the cosmos. They are akin to a sapling; there are roots, but they are fragile and not yet established. With each bite of this fruit the roots become stronger, creating a true foundation from which to view the world.

3. OUT OF THE GARDEN & INTO THE DESERT

"So the Lord God banished him from the garden of Eden, to till the ground from which he had been taken."
Genesis 3:23

Adam and Eve – Beginning the Journey

After eating the forbidden fruit, Adam and Eve are not only aware of their nakedness, but are expelled from the garden. This is an entirely different world in many fundamental ways. Adam and Eve not only see themselves as separate from their environment, but they also recognize that the world outside of Eden is not the paradise they had been accustomed to. This is the source of many new feelings for Adam and Eve - feelings that rise out of a sense of loss— the fall from paradise.

This is where the knowledge of good and evil soaks into Adam and Eve's perspectives of the world and permeates their consciousness. In the Garden of Eden, even after eating the apple, they were not fully aware of the harshness, struggles, or negativities of the life inevitably to come, but now there is no denying them. Adam and Eve experience the coldness of the winter and clothe themselves to keep warm and to cover up their nakedness. Because of such realizations emanating from their newly acquired ego-consciousness, they are now more aware of the existence of their flesh, for Adam and Eve recognize that the light of childhood is now shrouded in matter.

This realization of the flesh leads Adam and Eve to a deeper understanding of their own mortality. From dust they came and to dust they shall return - and now they begin to understand what this actually means - it is a new reality. And then they become aware of pain, of the need for survival, the process of aging, the harshness of life in the dessert, and separation from the garden. Adam and Eve now understand that death is a certainty, and this is a source of real sorrow.

Deep sorrow is not only inspired by their new realization of death, but also from the feeling that they have lost their life in paradise, the inevitability of change and impermanence, and the prospect of hard work and hard times. Adam and Eve experience the darkest sadness that I could imagine a human being might feel, for they were actually *in* paradise and enjoyed, without toil, the spiritual fruits that God had provided. They experienced the beauty, peace and harmony of the earth, animals and plants. They did not have a care in the world, for everything was provided for and perfect. But now, they are in a much different situation and know for certain that Eden has been lost and will never again be open to them. This is exactly what is happening in the soul life of the child! They have been thrown out into the desert and they are scared and afraid.

Not only is sorrow felt for the first time, but also betrayal. They feel that paradise was an entitlement and its retraction is a source of great anger. They are under the assumption and expectation that both the Creator and creation were perfect, unaffected by entropy. It is the illusion of paradise before the forbidden fruit that allows them to feel forsaken, and/or possibly set up by a God that can apparently make mistakes.

With this going on within their hearts, Adam and Eve struggle to transform their lives in order to survive and nourish themselves. The fruit provided by God is nowhere to be seen. God said to them while still in the garden:

> You will get your food from it (the earth) only by labor all the days of your life; it will yield thorns and thistles for you. You will eat of the produce of the field, and only by the sweat of your brow will you win your bread until you return to the earth; for from it you were taken. (3:17-19) [5]

Adam and Eve are now living the reality that God foreshadowed with this proclamation. Their inevitable future of self-reliance through practical activities becomes clear to our former inhabitants of the garden. They know they must tend to the soil in order to grow their own foods and nourish themselves, for they can no longer eat of Eden's fruit.

The world outside of Eden is vast compared to what was held within the garden gates. They are no longer held

---

[5] Oxford University, *Oxford Study Bible* (New York: Oxford University Press, 1992), 14

within the warm, safe confines of Eden, but are instead sitting exposed in the middle of the wilderness outside the gates. This brings the experience of fear - for the animals, landscapes and elements are not the same and familiar ones they had known in the garden. Now they can suffer, feel pain, and even face death, as attacks from predators, fatal falls, and overexposure to the elements are a constant possibility. This is the end of everything they knew, and the beginning of everything else that is to come. It is the fall from grace, and for our children, it is the moment the previously mentioned 'stream of change' takes its plunge into the earth.

Death & Sorrow – A New Understanding

Just like Adam and Eve, the child who is going through the nine-year change has to leave their own garden - the garden of childhood - because of a new awareness blossoming within them. This is an awareness of the birth of *ego-consciousness*. The awareness of ego-consciousness means the departure from childhood. Hermann Koepke wrote much on the nine-year change and gives this insight:

> How do children experience this transition? A trace of sadness in their eyes; their gait is heavier than before, and they have become more sensitive. They become aware that their world, in which they felt so fully at home, has become strange to them. From time to time, they want to withdraw from it entirely. They are puzzled by the separation between themselves and the world; their father, their mother, and their friends now stand outside the circle of their own world. They long to return; they long to be understood and loved.[6]

---

[6] Koepke, Hermann *Encountering the Self* (New York: Anthroposophical Press, 1989), 78

The child is now conscious of loss, or death--the death of the flesh, the loss of paradise, and the passing of the unconsciousness of childhood.

An element now enters the child's consciousness that wasn't there before, and this is the awareness of human mortality. The child becomes aware of mortality and the inevitable death that all living things must face. It may be the case that a child who is still in 'the garden' has experienced death and has even asked about it, but it is not until after they have eaten the fruit that they can ever *identify* with death and have a true awareness of their own mortality.

One can only become conscious of *losing* the Self when they have become conscious of *having* a Self. The child can now really delve into the idea of death in a realistic way and with a cognitive, even abstract element from their feeling life. This type of cognition separates the child from their feelings of togetherness, and gives them the feeling of being alone. However, this loneliness is a great gift. It grows very fine and subtle feelings that were not possible before, and this is quite a powerful and necessary experience. It is through loneliness that the child can become aware of her ego. The child gains this new-found ego-consciousness, meaning that they are more within *themselves* and less apart of the world around them. This is a time when the theme of death often makes it's way into a child's play-life, or when questions about death are asked.

Then, the world changes from a beautiful garden to a harsh desert, infinitely expansive, and utterly unknown. The child feels alone and forsaken, for the world is not the utopia she had once believed it to be. There is a realized separation and a real sense of loss within the child, which can manifest itself in many different behaviors. The feelings that arise in the aftermath of "the fall", serve to accentuate the Self and begin to shape it. This accentuation can take an assertive, or even an aggressive form. Children will sometimes feel great insecurity, and want to stay close to parents and home. Irrational fears may be present. Many children have nightmares during this time and can exhibit a great deal of anxiety. They can now see that the adults in their lives are capable of making mistakes, and this can be a frightening proposition. It will often inspire anger from the child, as their trusted source is no longer flawless, and they will point this out with vigor in an effort to show their new sense of justice. They will often question the authority of adults who are now seen as human beings who can fail—just like the vast, harsh desert outside the gates of Eden prove that God has created something imperfect - something less than paradise.

Everything now becomes flawed compared to the paradise that has been lost and this is a problematic state for the child. Essentially, Adam and Eve are orphaned and isolated, and angry about it. Before, people and things held a magical quality for the child, but now they see the inherent flaws that reside in everything. Some children will point out how foul, wrong, and alien the world has become. Some children will withdraw and actually be as distant as they feel

— expressing themselves nonverbally from the secure confines of the quietude and solitude. The young child learns and expresses herself through imitation. This is how we teach children in the kindergarten – we model the behavior we want the children to have. It does no good to reason with them! After the age of seven, this quality is still present, but it begins to change. At this time the child begins to emulate, in addition to imitate. It is a gradual process until they begin the nine-year change. At this time the age of imitation is over and they are now free to make their own decisions – hopefully the child has an example to follow, and they will emulate the behavior they believe is correct. It is this assertion of ego that will assist the child in beginning to individuate through consciousness.

The child can also give form and order to their new reality in much the same way Adam and Eve did; namely through farming. Farming is practiced and discussed in Waldorf schools for the purposes of showing the children how we survive and nourish ourselves, so they may begin to feel at home on earth. Farming provides a picture of how a person can produce physical nourishment for themselves through hard work. The practical art of farming provides an experience of how humans cannot only provide physical nourishment for themselves, but the archetype also correlates to how we provide ourselves with emotional, intellectual, and spiritual sustenance. The fruit no longer hangs from the tree—we must toil to create it.

Cain & Abel – Light & Shadow

*"If you do well, you hold your head up;
if not, sin is a demon crouching at the door;
it will desire you, and you will be mastered by it."*
Genesis 4:7

The feelings and the behaviors of the child are not the light filled gestures of childhood—a dreamy state of sparkly-eyed wonderment. The child's gesture is now somewhat shadowy, curious, and strangely awake. They may begin to tell lies, in order to test you. Some become secretive, realizing for the first time that you, the parent, don't magically know everything already. It can be a time for pranks as well. On the darker end of the spectrum, some children express rage and anger and can be quite difficult to manage. All these signs indicate that the child has encountered their shadow side. This aspect of the nine -year change can be expressed clearly through the archetypes in the story of Cain and Abel.

Adam and Eve give birth to two sons, Cain and Abel. The two boys grow up together and forge a very close connection—as if they were one person—and are virtually inseparable. As they progress into their lives they must separate, or diverge in order to provide nourishment for the family. Cain works the land and yields the fruits of the earth, whereas Abel tends to the flocks and cares for the animals. The two men sweat buckets to tame the world into which they were cast and begin to work towards recreating Eden and discovering how to provide for themselves.

Cain and Abel know that God is still watching over them and blessing their deeds, so they offer up a sacrifice of thanks and praise to honor God for the grace given to them.

> In due season Cain brought some of the fruits of the earth as an offering to the Lord, while Abel brought the choicest of the first born of his flock. The Lord regarded Abel and his offering with favor, but not Cain and his offering. Cain was furious and he glowered.[7]

Cain allowed his anger to overcome him, and he invites Abel to go out into the country with him. Cain attacks and murders his brother. Abel's blood soaks into the earth and

---

[7] Oxford University, *Oxford Study Bible* (New York: University Press, 1992), 14

he cries out to God, who then questions Cain and convicts him of murder. Cain is banished from the country of his family and must wander the earth. He is ordered to hide from the presence of God, but first, he is given a mark so that no one will kill him for the sin he has committed.

Cain came face to face with his shadow, and he did not have the ability to tame it. This story shows the children that we all struggle with our shadows, but also warns of what can happen if we don't exert self-control.

There is a notable symbolic difference between Cain's and Abel's sacrifices--one is of the plant world (etheric) and the other is of the animal world (astral). Abel's offering is favored by God, or the Self, for it is time to begin tending to the freeing up of the astral body from the cosmos. This is the task of the child from 7-14, whereas the etheric should be extracted from the cosmos already thus ending the stage of imitation and entering the newer stage of emulation. The Self recognizes this and honors it.

The Two Selves – Shadow & Light

*"While growing up, the ego is actually strengthened by resisting certain undesirable alter egos or morally ugly shadow forces.
This is a necessary endeavor, as the young ego needs firming up."*
Eugene Pascal Jung to Live By

The archetypal images present in the story of Cain and Abel are the same archetypal truths present in the nine-year change. Cain and Abel represent the duality of the child – light and shadow.

Upon realizing this duality, the child turns away from the light they have always known and for the first time, notices the shadow streaming outward from their feet. The ego of every human being has a shadow within it, and the nine-year change is the first true encounter with it. The child stands facing the shadow and eventually, the shadow overtakes their consciousness, just as Cain overtakes Abel. The child must allow this shadow side to exist, just as God allows the shadow to exist by allowing Cain to keep his life.

The child may fight this process, but it must happen. Each human soul contains both sides, and resistance to one is resistance to the other.

Jung taught that hate directed at our shadow will only elicit an odious response from it in return, creating more unnecessary chaos and turmoil in our lives. This consciousness and acceptance of the shadow Self is the mark the God bestows on Cain. Once they realize that it's there, children dwell with their shadow for a time and journey deeper into the Self—just as Cain is cast out further into the wilderness, the land, the Self. The child must learn to manage and transform these impulsive, angry, violent and animalistic tendencies.

At times, they will fail to exert control over these feelings of shadow and these feelings will come tumbling out. Full-blown temper tantrums are not uncommon at this age. They can also lose their control at school with peers and fights may occasionally occur. Hopefully, these more troublesome behaviors are sporadic, and short-lived.

Tubal Cain - Transformation & Home Life

Cain left the presence of God and built a great city, and his descendants multiplied. Some of these descendants carry on the impulsive and violent tendencies of their father, while some of his children become cunning craftsmen. The later obtain great wisdom and knowledge by which they subdue and transform the deed of Cain through the practical arts. There is Jabal, who tames the wild beast to serve in earthly toil and provide food. There is Jubal, who opens himself to the music of heaven, not heard since Eden, and brings it to the Earth--providing moments of beauty and lightness to ease the shadowy heaviness of the desert. but one stands out as a shining archetype of transformation. This descendant is named Tubal Cain.

Tubal Cain is a talented blacksmith who holds the light of God within him. He makes his living forging the strongest implements of battle that anyone has ever seen, and his reputation spreads far across the land. Over many years Tubal arms many men and his tools shed oceans of blood. Tubal is deeply disturbed by his contribution to so much death and suffering, so he seeks to reverse and correct the ills that his creations produce.

Tubal Cain takes every weapon that he has made from around his workshop and throws them into the forge. He melts them down and merges the metals together while his hammer rings and the red sparks explode out in all directions. When he is finished, Tubal dunks the shaped metal into the cooling water and after the steam clears, he beholds the very first metal plough-share. It is interesting to note that the iron content in the blood steadily increases as we grow older—the child works with iron, just as Tubal Cain did.

The plough transforms the nation, for it makes the art of farming easier and people no longer need to fight over the resources of the land. The violence and impulsiveness created by the sword and war is transformed into the labor and rhythm created by the plough and farming. New achievements and a way to be useful seem to lead the way out of such a problematic state.

Tubal finds meaning in the plough, for it tames and transforms the harsh desert and brings the world a little closer to the garden-like Eden. From the story of Tubal rises the third-grade farming block. While some type of work is customary throughout the entire year (as I mentioned earlier, Adam and Eve had to learn this work and so we bring it to the children earlier in the school year as well), this is when a visit to a working farm is of great value. One Waldorf school community I have been apart of is lucky enough to have a farm still powered by horses, to which the children can visit and work. An overnight trip where they can rise at dawn and really come to an understanding of what it takes to sustain oneself in this way, feeds the soul development of the nine to ten year old.

It is also wonderful if the responsibilities in the home can increase during this time. Hopefully, your child has had some kind of chore responsibility for several years now, but the nine-year old can really take up a new level of work. Not only are they capable of it now, but work will foster a sense of accomplishment. Children are so vulnerable at this time, and they are really not sure if they will find a place in the world for themselves. Setting them with tasks they can complete will assure them that there is a place to be had. If they can contribute within the constructs of the family, then they will be able to contribute beyond. It is an opportunity for the child to transform their irrational behavior and find redemption.

While Tubal exemplified true transformation, the wickedness of the world continued to increase and, despite the contribution of Tubal Cain, God feels that the earth needs to be purified so that the righteous may repopulate the earth.

Noah & the Flood – Self - Sufficiency

*"Noah was a righteous man,
the one blameless man of his time,
and he walked with God."*
Genesis 6:9

In a land filled with wickedness, Noah is the light among the shadows. He dwells in the favor of God and is chosen by God to be the human who will repopulate the earth with goodness. God instructs Noah that he is to build a great ark that will save him and his family from the great flood that God will initiate. Noah is also instructed to bring two of every living creature and all of the food of the earth that is good to eat. Being a man who 'walks with God', Noah fulfills God's request to its completion.

On the very day that Noah finishes the tasks that God has given him, "all the springs of the great deep burst out, the windows of the heavens were opened, and rain fell on the earth for forty days and forty nights" (7:11-12). The earth floods and everything that lives upon it perishes in the inescapable influx of waters from all directions—only Noah and the inhabitants of the ark survive. Eventually the rains come to a halt, the springs of the great deep cease their flowing, the sun emerges once again, and God causes a wind to blow over the earth so that the waters begin to subside. To ensure that safety is again to be had, Noah sends a raven out to survey the landscape and report back. This raven never returns. Not being discouraged, Noah then sets out a dove. The dove returns with an olive leaf, showing to Noah that there is again earth upon which to stand. Noah now knows that the earth touches the sky once more.

Just as God directs Noah to build the ark to ensure his salvation from the flood, the child is building her own inner vessel in which to weather these turbulent storms. This "vessel" is built as the child learns to listen to her inner voice, just as Noah was able to hear the voice of God within himself. With the tools gained from the story of Tubal, the child is able to construct the ark that will sustain her through the storm. And after the storm, the child sends out her own raven and dove.

Noah's raven is a representation of the child's shadow, which when used does not produce the desired results. When the child calls upon the dove (her light), this bears success. It is through trial and error that the child can see the results of utilizing both of these sides of herself. Giving into shadow produces nothing, while radiating light brings forth green growth. This particular realization is vitally important for the child. It is one of the first instances in which they come to internalize 'right and wrong". This internalization is fostered by loving authority. This sense of justice must grow organically, and not be forced upon them. Nothing that anyone else can offer will ever 'take root' within them. They may come to know what is 'right and wrong', but they will never love dead rules as much as rules that are a living reality within them. Just as Confucius once said, "He who merely knows right principles is not equal to him who loves them."

This internalization of 'right and wrong' is a process. While the child has an innate sense of the reciprocal nature of the universe, or karmic rhythms, they must test these rules out. If the authority presence in their life is loving, but firm, then the child will come to realize that they will catch more flies with honey, as parents and teachers provide antipathetic stance toward vinegar.

After the flood subsides, Noah is rewarded by God for his faithfulness, and is given governance over all the plants and animals and sets a rainbow across the sky. Because the child has built a sound ship, weathered the storm, and remained true to Self, they are rewarded too. They now know they are capable of dealing with the storms of life, believing that at the end, they too, will be rewarded with a rainbow - a promise that a flood of this magnitude will never happen again.

The Tower of Babel – Unabashed Arrogance

*"Let us build ourselves a city
and a tower with its top in the heavens
and make a name for ourselves,
or we shall be dispersed over the face of the earth."*
Genesis 11:4

After the child has mastered ship-building, they have a new sense of accomplishment — however, this leads to false security. This is when the nine-year old seems to think they know everything – and oh, how they enjoy telling us this! Parents are reminded of when their child was a toddler and discovered the words "no!", and "I can do it myself!". Teachers inwardly smile (while we are also endlessly frustrated) when half the class suddenly seems to think they understand the world better than the teacher. Because they have found success for the first time since the stream of change has taken its dive, children now think they will never fail - life will always be rainbows. And just when the surrounding adults can't stand the egotism any longer, the child faces another challenge and it all comes crashing down again - this is expressed in the archetype of the Tower of Babel.

The people of Noah go forth and settle the land, creating a new civilization. To mark the time and space, the people begin to build a great tower that will reach to the heavens. However, this is not God's plan. This is not the land they were intended for, and God comes down and makes it so the people can no longer understand one another – he confuses their language. They lose their power of communication, and their plans for the tower are thwarted. The people are scattered over the face of the earth.

God saw that these plans for a 'stairway to heaven', would eventually lead the people away from Him. Such a stairway is not for humanity to build – only God has the right to construct such a creation. God sees that the desire to build this tower is ego driven, and halting its construction shows God's desire for the people to learn humility. It is interesting to note that the people constructed the tower out of brick and tar, instead of stone and mortar - man-made materials as opposed to God-made. Although this tower was touted as a 'stairway to heaven', it was really a demonstration of the people's abilities and achievements - not a monument to God.

The ego-consciousness that is taking root within the child can sometimes grow faster than the Self is prepared to work with. This egotism is represented in the tower. The child feels as though they have mastered a new language, have built a ship, and now they know all they need to know! They have the power to communicate on all matters – just as the people of Babel initially had one language in which all could communicate. This language is a complex 'feeling language', and they really do not know how to interpret it, although they sure think they do, since they have encountered the flood and survived. Because the child believes they have mastered all that they must master, they are fooled into thinking the difficult times are past, and that now they can return to the garden. They get comfortable - then the Self comes in and like God, confuses the language further, so that the child now realizes they do not have the skills to truly understand. This obliterates the ability to settle into a comfortable, new land. The child has *encountered* the Self, but they are far from *knowing* the Self.

Although the child has far to go before she is fluent in her new language of feeling, she does have an evolving consciousness surrounding it. She is building up news walls, brick by brick. Noah's people believed that building a new civilization would make a name for them in God's eyes, and the child secretly longs to make a name for her new-found Self as well – but the name must fit, and finding the correct one is a process. This is a time when children often insist on being called a name other then what has been typically used. Sometimes this is their given name (wanting to be called Thomas, instead of Tommy), but the child may also desire something completely new. Foreign sounding names from fairytales are a consistent favorite, or a beloved book or television character. This 'trying on' of alternative egos allows the child to take up characteristics that they do not yet possess, but desire.

Eventually, the child realizes that they aren't prepared to settle this new land alone, that they can't return to the garden, that the tower is not going to be built, and they again agree to a bit of guidance. It is time to move on. So, out into the wilderness of Self they are cast once again - out into the shadows. Parts of the child become the different peoples of history, scrapped across the different colors of soil, constructing civilizations in the wilderness of the Self. These widespread new ego impulses now exist within the child—the child may find them, or they may find the child. These impulses represent a diversification that will feed the individuation process. Either way, the child will not be conscious of these impulses; they will merely display them in the coming years. From the methodical Egyptians, to the dualistic Persians, to the transcendental Hindus, to the eclectic Greeks; the child possesses the consciousness of all humanity throughout time and will encounter the echoes of the impulses of these ancient peoples in years to come—just as Abram does when he visits Egypt.

4. THE PROMISED LAND

*"Leave your own country, your kin,
and your father's house, and go to a country
that I will show you.
I shall make you into a great nation."*
Genesis 12:1-2

God's Covenant with Abram – Anticipating the Future

After God scatters the people over the earth in all directions, he approaches a man named Abram and offers him a promise. The promise is for a land that shall belong to Abram and all of his descendants, so Abram gathers his family and their possessions and they travel out to settle this new land – the land of Canaan. Abram and his family are grateful, and build an altar meant to invoke the name of God. After some time, the land becomes stricken with famine, and Abram and his family are forced to go to Egypt for some time. While there, Abram observes this great civilization and the complexities of its government, beliefs, farming, building and rituals.

Abram learns many things while spending time in Egypt, but is eventually asked to return to the land from whence he came. Abram and his family return to Canaan, bringing with them Abrams's nephew, Lot. They return to the site of the altar, and begin to set up their tents and prepare to settle the land, yet it becomes clear that the land and water supply are not enough to support both families and herds. So, Abram says to Lot, "There must be no quarreling between us, or between my herdsmen and yours; for we are close kinsmen. The whole country is there in front of you. Let us part company" (13:8-9)[8]. Abram gives Lot the first choice of land—whatever direction Lot goes, Abram agrees to go the other way. Lot looked around and saw how well-watered the whole plain around Jordan was; all the way to Zoar it was like the Garden of the Lord. (13:10)[9] Lot goes east and settles this fertile plain near the city of Sodom, and Abram travels west and settles deeper into the land of

---

[8] Ibid, 22

[9] Ibid, 22

Canaan. God tells Abram that the land he is settling is truly the land which has been promised to him.

Eventually, there is war in the fertile plain that Lot had chosen and Lot, his family, and all of his herds are taken prisoner—as well as the other people and herds of the plain (the people of Sodom and Salem). A fugitive brings this information to Abram and at once, Abram gathers together retainers (servants) and men born in his household to rescue Lot's family and their herds. Abram's men accomplish this and return Lot and all of his possessions, as well as the other imprisoned peoples and their animals to the land near Sodom and Salem.

The king of Sodom and the king of Salem go out to meet Abram in the plain. Melchizedek, the king of Salem, comes with food, wine and a blessing—for he is a priest of God. Abram gives the priest a 'tithe' of the booty recovered for his generosity and his most graceful blessing. The king of Sodom makes a greedy proposal that if Abram gives him the people, then Abram can have the herds. Abram is offended and refuses to accept anything from this wicked man. God speaks once again to Abram in a vision. He [says], "Don't be afraid, Abram; I am your shield. Your reward will be very great." (15:1)[10]

Abram tells God that he is concerned that he and his wife, Sarai have not yet produced an heir, and he fears that the children of the slaves of his household will inherit his possessions. God replies, these men "will not be your heirs; your heir will be of your own body." (15:4) Abram puts faith in what God has put forth to him as righteousness. After several years, God appears to Abram and tells him that he will be the father of many nations; therefore he will no longer be Abram, but Abraham. God also says:

> 'I shall make you exceedingly fruitful; I shall make nations from you, and kings shall spring from you. I shall maintain my covenant with you and your descendants after you, generation after generation, an everlasting covenant: I shall be your God, yours and your descendants. As a possession for all time I shall give you and your descendants after you the land in which you are now aliens.'[11]

---

[10] Ibid, 23

[11] Ibid, 23

Shortly after this, a son is born to Abraham and Sarai—her name changes too, for she is now the 'mother of many nations', and she is now known as Sarah, and they give the child the name that God has provided - Isaac.

The Future Realized

"Out of ancient humanity, from which the dim beginning of its consciousness has read its eternal verities in the stars, comes a party traveling by no known compass. Out of the human race, which knows in its bones that all of its striving must end in death, comes a leader who says he has been given an impossible promise. Out of the mortal imagination comes a dream of something new, something better, something yet to happen, something—in the future."
Thomas Cahill, *The Gifts of the Jews*

Abram is the archetype of the ego-consciousness, which is beginning to understand what the future holds. Children should feel that the work they are doing is preparing them for the future. They can see that the world is flawed, but within this imperfect place, they are capable of worthy achievements. The world is in a constant struggle between good and evil, light and shadow; the same struggle that is being waged within themselves. Both the child and the world are capable of shadow, but also of great wonders and beauty. It is hoped that the better one is at listening to one's inner voice, the brighter the light. This is the lesson of Abram — the ability to let your inner light guide you through difficult times. When children realize this as a possibility, they can become much more comfortable in their new reality, and can settle into the goodness they find around them.

Children are now beginning to reacquaint themselves with the goodness of the world and humanity. They are noticing, hopefully, in the adults around them that people are capable of resurrecting the garden within themselves and the world. Yet, it is not the same garden of pure light that they came from, for consciousness has exposed the shadows. However, consciousness will also uncover the depths of existence - the light within the shadow, *and* the shadow within the light. This interplay of light and shadow are the shades of gray, and the spectrum of color, found within humanity. The child is experiencing a new desire for this ego-consciousness so that guidance to the Promised Land can be received.

As in previous stories, an altar is built. Once again, there is a building up of scattered pieces, representing the shattered pieces within the child. They must again build a new vision of the Self from what they have thus far encountered through ego-consciousness. These are markers found along the way that represent a significant realization - growth in ego-consciousness and a deeper encounter with Self (God). This cycle will continue into the future, and just as the new descendants of Abraham will evolve and obtain an ever growing consciousness of God, the child's ego-consciousness will grow to behold a deeper cognition of Self.

This story represents a worldly patriarch's trust in a disembodied voice. When all things are lost, the voice within can still be a guide. God's promise to Abram represents the promise that the child will one day find their 'promised land' and be at home in their body upon the earth while guided by the Self, the ego, the grace of God.

The child encounters the promised land within them, and they see that it is stricken by a famine of sorts. The land is uninhabitable at the moment and so, like Abram seeking refuge in Egypt, they look out into the world for sustenance and an example of how to survive. They just do not yet have the skills necessary to cultivate on their own, so the child really looks deeply into how we sustain ourselves by sheltering, clothing, and feeding.

They really want to know where these necessities come from, so they must be guided, once again, to the farm— to where the seed and the soil meet to make bread; to the sheep and its wool to see where their sweater comes from; to the first shelters of humanity. This point in the journey is a great place for a 'building block' in the curriculum, if not done as a year long specialty class.

The children envision, plan, and execute an outdoor structure that could truly sustain them. It is nice if the children can also create something that will add value to the school. An outdoor playhouse that the kindergarten can enjoy is a wonderful project. Many Waldorf classes also hold a 'sheep to shawl' block during this time to connect the children to this desire to understand the process behind our necessities. They travel to a farm to see the sheep in person, then can help with the shearing. They can brush, card, spin, and dye the wool, creating yarn which they will then use in handworks. Gardening, followed by a harvest can be done at school or at home to further this connection to the necessities of life.

While the school projects are usually loved dearly by the children, projects done at home can sometimes be a struggle. Over and over again the child will deny the adults in their lives, only to return to them for more life lessons, and more skill work. They will oscillate between not wanting anything to do with the 'adult work' going on, and then taking it up with a determined hand. The children learn to survive from the adults around them, as Abram learned to survive from his time in Egypt, for he benefited in Egypt by the gifts of Pharaoh and observing the ways of the more established civilization. In many ways we adults are Egypt, Pharaoh, and its more established ways—the child turns to us for wisdom in action - for a strong ego at work. And whether or not they enjoy every moment of it, children need guidance. Firm and loving guidance.

Abram & Lot – Out with the Old and in with the New

After they learn some skills that will ensure their survival, back to the land of promise the child goes and, once there, realizes there is not enough land for both the Abram ego and the Lot ego. The Abram ego is the present Self, whereas the Lot ego is the immature ego still longing for youth—the child has grown out of this ego. When given the choice of what land to inhabit, Lot chooses the land that resembles 'the garden of the Lord'— this ego longs for the past, and chooses the land that looks like the one he came from. The more mature Abram, puts faith in God, trusting that this inner voice with make the right decision — this ego is ready for the future. Children also begin to listen to the Self, and it guides them with a promise of hope. They hope that through an act of faith, coming from a virtually unknown voice, they will be blessed and continue to flourish upon the earth. The flow of the 'stream of change' is beginning to slow up, gathering in the lowness, soon to be building up pressure to rise upward—this is the 'voice' inside of them. It is also a *feeling* within them and is the future of thinking.

Here there is a separation of the newer ego-consciousness that can hear the Self from the older ego-*unconsciousness* of childhood—it is literally *the* archetype for "*Nova ex veteris*", or, "the new must be born out of the old". Just as God leads Abram to the Promised Land without Lot, the child turns from childhood and treks deeper into the new Self with less of the childhood impulse tagging along. The child is beginning to work towards the future and the strengthening and maturation of the ego facilitates this.

Sodom & Gomorrah - Questioning Authority

Sodom and Gomorrah hold a couple of important archetypes for the nine-year change. First, the cities of Sodom and Gomorrah represent an attempt at rebuilding the garden - an attempt to return to Eden. During the nine-year change there will be many points at which the child will try to re-create what they once had. They desperately miss the unconscious, blissful state of childhood and much time is spent in denial. These attempts to revert to childhood are not sustainable, as the ego is now awake and will not retreat. Each time the child denies growth and flees for Eden, or an 'Eden-esque' land, the ego comes in and destroys this hope, just as God destroys Sodom and Gomorrah. We can also see Sodom and Gomorrah as a representation of childish behaviors and manifestations, which are no longer allowed. Behaviors such as temper tantrums and name-calling are no longer tolerated, and will eventually receive punishment.

The story of Sodom and Gomorrah yields another striking archetype that correlates to the child's new courage and ability to successfully question authority, which is sponsored by their ever-growing consciousness and objectivity in observation. In *The Gifts of the Jews,* Thomas Cahill writes:

> When god reveals his plan for the destruction of Sodom and Gomorrah, Avram attempts to reason with him: "Will you really sweep away the innocent along with the guilty?" By questioning God, who has been gradually revealing his awesome grandeur to Avram, the patriarch exhibits striking courage, a courage that will reappear in his descendants throughout ages to come.[12]

The recognition of a flawed authority has now evolved into the ability to question and reason with it, and the courage that makes it all possible is brought to them through the strengthening ego. The ego is becoming ever more conscious of the Self, with its feeling and thinking. With this new ability to reason, Abram even attempts to barter a deal with God.

Abram debates his Lord into sparing these wicked cities if he can find a minimum number of righteous people

---

[12] Cahill, Thomas *The Gift of the Jews* (New York: Anchor Books, 1998), 70

within them. He starts out with a high number (50 people), easing God into the lower number of 10 people. There is cunningness at work within Abram, as Abram is aware that the numbers of the righteous are falling. This same cunningness is present within the child. The child is not only pointing out the imperfections of the world, but they are now questioning, debating and gaining a deeper knowledge. They will try this new ability to be cunning with the authority figures in their life.

Abram truly represents the child's expanding self-awareness—he built more altars than anyone before him, taking the pieces to build up the whole. And it is probably true that Abram's altars kept improving with each new one, like the child's ego continues to gain more uprightness, form and stability. The more they listen to the voice of the Self, the greater Self awareness becomes, and through the understanding of feeling and thought, the more blessed the child is by the Self.

A New Name - Individuation

> *"Avraham's relationship to God became the matrix of his life, the great shaping experience. From voice to vision to august potentate, Avraham's understanding of God grew ever larger."*
> Thomas Cahill, *The Gifts of the Jews*

Abram is transformed when God changes his name. He is given the name Abraham, for he will be the patriarch of many great nations. A person entering a new relationship or achieving a new status may receive an appropriate new name. The child is now realizing the potential of their own autonomy, which can be both exhilarating and uncertain. Knowing that the Self will guide them (but only if they are open enough to hear its voice), the child must learn how to keep the ego open and hear the Self - like Abraham was open to the voice of God. They will need to observe a strong ego-consciousness at work within the adults around them in order to see a living picture of the promised land.

After God gives Abraham his new name, God again makes the promise of land, along with other new promises. God swears to maintain this covenant of land, *or Self*, for the generations of evolving ego-consciousness to come. The child sees that this promise is guaranteed to the ego, and that this blessing shall be carried into the future—the ego strives to encounter and reflect the Self. Also, God proclaims that he will be the God of all of Abraham's descendants, just as the Self is the God of the ever-evolving ego. Furthermore, God asserts that the descendants will rise up as kings, or monarchs. The word 'monarch', broken down— *monos*=alone & *archein*=to rule, stands for the acquiring of more self-responsibility--the governance of ego. If the ego can obtain the strength needed, the child may now feel the first stirrings of their own inner monarch - the ability to govern themselves more autonomously.

It is apparent that the relationship with the Self, like the relationship between God and Abraham, is giving the child a sense of inner strength, confidence and trust in the life that is to come. The only enemy now is the solipsism of the ego, or the attempted reversion to the unconsciousness of childhood. This may keep the child from accepting the ever-growing need for self-responsibility. The child needs a strong ego-consciousness in order to interpret feelings, allowing them to then interpret and understand the feelings that are rising up within the Self. For this to happen they must give up their childhood and the selfishness it allowed - this is a pivotal sacrifice.

The Sacrifice of Isaac – Letting Go

> *"Take your son, your one and only son Isaac whom you love, and go to the land of Moriah. There you shall offer him as a sacrifice."*
> *(Genesis 22:2)*

Abraham and Isaac become very close as father and son. Abraham feels a great joy in his heart, having an heir to the land, just as God has promised. His relationship with God is deepening, and he is putting a great deal of faith in his Lord, but one day Abraham is put to the test. God tells Abraham that he is to take his only son to the heights of Mount Moriah and offer Isaac up as a sacrifice. Abraham prepares for the sacrifice without any debate with God.

Abraham gathers all that is needed for the sacrifice, including Isaac, but just before they get to their destination, Isaac asks his father where the sheep is for the offering. Abraham replies, that God will provide him with a sheep for the sacrifice. He and Isaac arrive at the place of which God has spoken, and Abraham builds an altar on which to offer his son. Abraham arranges the wood, binds Isaac and places him on top of the wood, and yields a knife high over his head. Just then, the angel of God calls to him from heaven.

The angel of God tells Abraham that Isaac will be spared by the grace of Abraham's own faith in God's command. He turns around and sees a ram with its horn tangled in a thick bush nearby, and he sacrifices the ram instead of his son. God has truly provided for, and blessed Abraham, for Abraham has proven his unconditional trust in God through his willingness to sacrifice his only son. God reiterates his promises to Abraham with a strong conviction —expanding upon the greatness of his blessings.

Isaac & the Ram - Sorting Through the Past

"Man sacrifices a great deal in order to become an ego conscious being."
A.C. Harwood, *The Recovery of Man in Childhood*

The story of Abraham's willingness to sacrifice Isaac represents the ego-consciousness of the child. It has grown to the point where it stands apart from its 'forefathers' (older, immature ego centers). The child is growing accustomed to their inner voice and is beginning to enjoy the benefits of ego struggles -consciousness and a new understanding of Self and the world. The voice of the Self is now finding a place within the child—literally the ego is incarnating into the child's body and the Self is recognizing this. Over time, Abraham's people feel less alien in their new land, just as the child is settling into their new world. The Self speaks to them as they become more conscious of the world around them, giving them a growing sense of safety, a sense of 'home'. This deepened relationship requires the ultimate sacrifice—the conscious willingness to sacrifice the unconsciousness of childhood.

There is a paradox that exists here. The child's very willingness to leave childhood behind is the gesture that gives the Self the ability to spare childhood, but not childhood in its entirety. The Self is comprised of both light and shadow, and so is the sacrificial passage of childhood. The duality of childhood can be expressed through the terms *childlike* and *childish*. These terms are subtle opposites, yet interwoven. Within the story, this duality is presented by Isaac and the ram; childlike behavior can be correlated to Isaac, whereas childishness is represented by the ram. Abraham's faith in God's request to kill Isaac is the very thing that saves Isaac, and God provides the ram. The child's trust in the Self allows the preservation of childlike tendencies, while sacrificing childishness.

The term childlike instantly calls up terms and phrases such as innocence, unconditional love, simplicity, compassion, feelings of oneness, reverence, wonderment, imagination, enthusiasm, spontaneity, joy, non-judgment and purity. All of the behaviors that offer light to the child and the people around them, all of the behaviors that bring us smiles and joy. Child*likeness* is the light of childhood.

When thinking of childishness, we are reminded of words and phrases like solipsism, self-centeredness, impulsiveness and selfishness. All of these behaviors cast shadows on the things around them, representing childishness—all of the behaviors that bring us grimaces and frustration. A temper tantrum inspired by spoiled, self-centered desires is not something that should survive past childhood—this ram must be sacrificed.

Both sides of childhood require a certain level of unconsciousness, but child*likeness* can be preserved within a growing ego-consciousness through experience, feeling, and memory. Jung tells us that whatever is given to us by the past is adapted to the possibilities and demands of the future. Childishness is tamed and cast out by the consciousness of action and consequence from past experience, for they are learning what is considered good and bad behavior from their parents and peers. This understanding is facilitated by *modeling* ego-consciousness in a healthy manner for the child. It is essential that the child receives such examples to properly guide them to the Self and confidently out into the world.

Digging Wells – Preserving the Past

> *"The child gradually learns to discern time,*
> *Piaget says, to discern past and present and future,*
> *and to reckon time. Yet the child is not thereby freed*
> *from the present, we could say,*
> *for he still lives largely in the moment."*
> John S. Dunne, Time and Myth

Isaac represents a new, transformed ego that possesses few of the remaining shadows of childhood. Later in life, Isaac goes out into the desert and digs wells in order to make the land habitable and fertile, so that he and his descendants may flourish. This is the contribution of Abraham's heir, and if the archetype is observed, it can be asserted that 'digging' can be correlated to the uncovering of the past, or memory itself. The faculty of memory is an essential condition of ego-consciousness. The child has been building up her ability to consciously experience and gain knowledge through memory, and now memory has evolved to the point where it is bringing new life to the promised land by uncovering the buried treasures of childlikeness.

The digging of wells - or the preservation of childhood's light, is the very act that gathers the life giving waters together. Water is the light brought by memory to the shadowy desert of struggle. As was mentioned before, the child will sort through the past and adapt the useful elements of childhood to the future, in order to evolve and grow. It is this revisiting of childlikeness that allows the survival of the eternal 'inner child', which will hopefully remain a conscious part of the Self for the remainder of life.

It is the inner child that brings the pure joy of living, the imagination to understand the universe, and the innocence that allows the child to reverence the Self—humbling the ego-consciousness to be open to the Self. These are the things that make the life of adults more blessed and wonderful. Not everything should be forgotten from childhood, for there is nourishment from childhood that brings life to the new land.

It is worth mentioning that this story also represents the experience of parents. During this pivotal moment in the child's life, each parent must allow this sacrifice of childhood. It is hard to give life to a child; to nurture and watch them grow, only to stand by while they struggle to emerge from the radiant wonder of childhood. Parents experience their own 'fall' through watching the child.

It is time to let the child travel their own path out into the wilderness of the world - the wilderness that lies both *within* and *around* them. Just as it is so important to not force the child into the change too soon (don't give that apple too early), it can also cause harm if the child is held behind. If she is not allowed to go at her own pace, then she may experience even greater struggles in trying to encounter the Self when she is older and not as equipped, or open, to manage this change. It would be like forcing a sprout back beneath the soil because we have become attached to the period between planting and the emergence of the plant. Let what must emerge grow out into the world.

Jacob & Esau

*"Two nations are in your womb,
two peoples going their own ways from birth.
One will be stronger than the other;
The elder shall be servant to the younger."*
(Genesis 25:23)

God blesses Isaac and his wife Rebecca, with twins. The two children press upon each other in the womb and bring Rebecca great discomfort. Unaware that she is carrying twins, Rebecca calls to God and asks him why she feels such pain. God explains that she has 'two great nations' in her womb that are already struggling to go their own ways. The first child to emerge possesses a reddish coloring and a 'cloak' of hair—he is named Esau. The second child immediately follows, holding on to the heel of Esau—he is named Jacob. The boys grow up and experience the world in different ways. Esau grows up to become a skillful hunter and outdoorsman, while Jacob lives quietly, staying close to home.

One day Esau returns from afar, exhausted and weakened from the harshness of the wilderness to find Jacob preparing a red broth. Esau asks his brother for a helping of the broth, feeling that he is on the brink of death, but Jacob will not give Esau any nourishment unless he agrees to trade his birthright. Esau replies that he is at death's door and so has no need of a birthright, Esau swears to give Jacob his birthright, and Jacob feeds his brother with red lentil broth, bread, and something to drink, and Esau goes on his way.

As time goes on, their father, Isaac, is losing his eyesight and feels that death is near, so he calls for Esau—so that he may bestow upon him his inheritance. Esau hears his father's call and says, "Here I am!" Isaac tells him to take his hunting gear out into the wilderness to get for him some wild game that Esau is to prepare as a savory dish--so that he may eat of it, and then bestow upon Esau his blessing. Esau gathers up his bow and quiver and treks into the wilderness, having no intention of keeping his word to Jacob. Rebecca overhears this and goes to Jacob with a plan to take the birthright from Esau.

Knowing that Isaac's sight has become dim, Rebecca knows that Isaac may be unaware of who is actually in front of him, so she instructs Jacob to take two goats from the flock and bring them to her so she can prepare the savory dish that Isaac enjoys. After Rebecca prepares the dish, she covers Jacob's hands and neck with goatskins so that to the touch, he will feel as hairy as his brother, Esau. Jacob is then dressed in Esau's finest garment, and he takes the meal to Isaac. Although Isaac, with his dim sight, recognizes the voice to be Jacob's, he touches the hands and is convinced that they are the hands of Esau, so Isaac eats the meal and drinks the wine. Before Isaac gives his blessing, he smells the clothes of his son, recognizes the smells of the wilderness, and bestows the blessing of the birthright upon Jacob.

Birthright & the Stream

"Jacob and Esau represent the dissolution of the old order and the coming of the new."
Roy Wilkinson, *Commentary on the Old Testament Stories*

It is at this point that we must again mention Steiner's 'stream of change'. Up until now the stream flowed downward into the underground channels and descended deeper into the darkness before coming to the nadir of the trough. At this point, the stream prepares its upward ascent back toward the surface. As the stream moves downward, it flows away from the light and into the shadowy darkness, but soon it will move upward, flowing away from the shadows and into the light of the world above. The story of Jacob stealing the birthright is exactly this moment when the stream reaches its deepest point, swirling and churning before it turns upward, preparing to move into the light of consciousness.

The story of Jacob and Esau must be compared to the story of Cain and Abel in order to see the archetypes in a clear manner and understand their relationship to Steiner's image of the stream. When the child consciously encounters the Self for the first time, it is through the shadow side, which is represented by Cain. Cain is the first born of Adam and Eve, therefore he possesses the birthright—the foundation of ego awareness. It is like the stream finding the opening into the underground channel and, plunging deeply inward, the ego encounters the depth of Self through the shadow.

It is necessary that the child encounter the Self through the shadow first, as the shadow is the birth of antipathy, thought, and ego-consciousness. If, through this change, the child encountered the light first, they would sympathetically bask in its slumbering, unconscious, rays and never really wake up. The shadow is transformative because it brings the child to actually recognize the light of childhood. It is only proper that Cain is the first-born of the two Selves, and also that the initial movement of Steiner's stream is downward.

In correlation to the duality of the Self as represented through the story of Cain and Abel—Cain being the shadow and Abel being the light—it is plain to see that Esau is representative of Cain and Jacob is representative of Abel. Jacob and Esau were struggling in Rebecca's womb over who would be first born, and the shadow, being the gateway to the Self up to this point, is the stronger side of the ego and emerges first—although the light is right on its heels, so to speak.

In relation to the stream, the waters have found their deepest descending point and begin to swirl chaotically, undulating between the forces of gravity and pressure as the flow of the waters ascend—between the unconscious and the conscious. Falling into gravity is a turbulent ride, but the rising up against gravity is a struggle requiring strength.

The two Selves are at a crossroads once again, and it is in this chaotic darkness that the sight of the ego is dimmed, much like the sight of Isaac, and the birthright is given over to the light in the confusion. Jacob brings forth a new impulse. There is a contrast here between strength and intelligence — Jacob obtains the birthright, and the light becomes the gateway to the Self.

Although the stream is beginning to move upward towards the light, it is still many channel twists and turns away, so although it may not be streaming in brightly, this new shift in direction will allow the child to see the light again. Within the child, there may exist a feeling, conscious or unconscious, that things are taking a different course.

At many points on this journey, the ego-consciousness turned around to behold the light of childhood moving away, but this is the last time this will happen before the child will begin to move into the light of adulthood, and turn around to behold the darkness of the cavern being left behind—the 'entry' light of childhood is replaced by the 'exit' light of adulthood. The Self is actually less connected with pre-life concerns and begins to work more towards post-life attainments.

From light to shadow and back to light again, it is the reciprocal relationship of light and darkness that lives everywhere and within everything in the known universe: day and night, life and death, wakefulness and sleep, ups and downs, growth and rest, expansion and contraction. Jacob will embrace the Self through the light, for he now possesses the birthright. The child's ego will now be born into the light of Self like the stream emerging earthward—the elements of childlikeness will aid in this rising. This will however, still require the ego to continually 'turn' and behold the shadow of the stream's cavern as it flows towards the surface, and the shadows of childhood (childishness and unconsciousness) must be encountered and worked with on the journey upward.

Wrestling in the Darkness with a Vision of the Light

*"Jacob, representing the new forces, is engaged in struggle all his life.
There is the conflict in the womb, for the birthright, over his wife,...[and] with beings from the spiritual world."*
Roy Wilkinson, Commentary on the Old Testament Stories

The Ladder

Just as Cain was cast out for his betrayal of Abel, so must Jacob leave for his crime against Esau—both 'wrong doings' were necessary. Cain killed Abel because Abel held God's favor, and now Esau wants to kill Jacob because Jacob has been given favor of the birthright. Cain is cast into the shadowy wilderness, but Jacob will flee into a wilderness that shall bring him a vision filled with light. He stops at a shrine to rest for the night.

> He took one of the stones there and, using it as a pillow under his head, he lay down to sleep. In a dream he saw a ladder, which rested on the ground with its top reaching to heaven, and angels of God were going up and down it.[13]

---

[13] Oxford University *Oxford Study Bible* (New York: Oxford University Press, 1992), 37

The child's ego-consciousness feels that the light is now the gateway, just as Jacob has his vision of a gateway one fateful night. He has the vision of a ladder rising to heaven, surrounded by light. Within the dream there is a new land—a land that promises a vision of light, and God promises this new land to Jacob. The child envisions their new land too, and through dreamy feeling and inspirations, they are guided to it. Abraham received a *promise* of the future, but Jacob receives a *vision*. The former is dependent on something external, while the latter comes from Self.

The ladder represents moving upward, like the stream rising from the depths, into a consciousness that gives a vision of higher knowledge through the light. Right now the child's thinking is feeling—feeling is the training ground for an ever-emerging capacity for thought, but this is still far off in the future. It was through movement that the child began to feel, it is through feeling that the child is beginning to think, and it will be through thinking that the adolescent begins to truly *know* the Self. Later on, the young adult and adult will venture into it, then come to comprehend it, and finally intellectualize its depths to attain a higher knowledge.

The child now puts forth their feeling into the world through the ego's interpretations. She is conscious of feeling and is gaining greater knowledge of herself through the strengthening of the ego. Her world of feeling is growing exponentially along with her consciousness of Self. *Feeling* is gaining depth and complexity, which feeds the life of thinking, of ego—expanding the child's knowledge of Self and world. Feeling is no longer a 'flood', for it is streaming, like the rushing of waters, from the Self with less resistance from the ego.

The ego now uses feeling to bring a deeper meaning to the world. The ego also uses experience to bring a deeper meaning to feeling. The child is more inside of themselves, looking out, than outside of themselves looking in. The stream is inside of the earth flowing towards the light, and no longer outside of the earth flowing into the cavernous shadow. Feeling gains brightness and is no longer so dark a venture.

Just a short while ago, the child was resisting the influx of strange new feelings, but now the child is embracing feeling more and more, and is willing to make sacrifices to follow her heart. Jacob sacrifices much of his time and efforts to obtain the woman that he loves so deeply—Rachel. He goes to great lengths and through his diligence, he achieves the fulfillment of his heart's desire. The ego offspring of Jacob's household is destined to inherit a greater consciousness of feeling, for they are to be nurtured in a household brought together through positive, light-filled feeling.

The child individuates through unique feeling experiences and by bringing will and consciousness to these experiences. After much struggling with his shadow, Jacob eventually takes ownership of his feelings, and asserts his ego to fulfill the needs of his heart — his love for Rachel. This new impulse will be passed on to his most cherished son.

This will be discussed later, through the archetypes of Joseph.

Wrestling with the Self

After the dream of the ladder, and his sacrifices to fulfill his desire for Rachel, Jacob encounters Esau for the very first time since he has taken his brother's birthright as the first born. The night before he encounters the shadowy Esau, Jacob wrestles with God. As a resolution, God gives Jacob a new name, *Israel*, and with this new name, comes greater identity.

As Jacob wrestles with God, the child wrestles with the Self, for the feelings of light are as new and alien as the feelings of shadow once were. The shadow Self is established first, like the roots of a flowering tree, and only after the roots have reached into the depths of darkness can the seed sprout into the light—conscious understanding of feelings sprout from the recognition of the unconscious roots of feelings through memory—here is where thinking is beginning to gestate. The roots are more established in the darkness of earth than the sprout emerging into the light of the world—remembering the root's movements teaches the sprout how to grow.

It is no accident that a tree resembles the saying, "as above, so below", for what is above ground mirrors what is below ground. Like the tree, the child will use the past to shape the future and use the future to shape the Self. The child struggles to sprout into a conscious knowledge of feeling exposed by the light - or future - towards which they now flow, using the nourishment that only the roots - or past - can provide them.

The child must now turn back around to the shadow, the past, the roots, so they can remember where they *were* in relation to where they *are*. This occurs because of the child's growing ability to remember the successive events leading up to where they stand—like tracing a shadow to one's own feet. Memory serves the child in recalling past struggles, so that they do not have to 'reinvent the wheel' as far as understanding and reacting to the feelings of the descent.

After wrestling with God, Jacob (Israel) encounters his brother, Esau, and fears that Esau will kill him for what he has done. Jacob offers an enormous amount of his possessions to Esau as recompense for the birthright. Esau kisses and throws his arms around Jacob. Jacob is surprised by his brother's forgiveness, but Esau has been through much and is himself blessed—he is a wise man for all of his struggles. Jacob insists that Esau take the offerings and his blessing as they part, and both return to their respective homes. On his way back to his father, Jacob builds an altar in Salem (Jerusalem). He enjoys his father in the remaining time he has left to live, and when Isaac dies, the brothers bury their father together.

Joseph - The First Born of Israel & Rachel

*"Because Joseph was a child of his old age,
Israel loved him best of all his sons,
And he made him a long robe with sleeves."*
(Genesis 37:3)

Joseph receives a special robe from his father, Israel. This robe is unlike any robe that Israel has bestowed upon his other sons, for it has long sleeves and is made of fine cloth. When Joseph's brothers see his new robe, they become stricken with a jealous anger and speak harshly about Joseph. Joseph stands alone as the favorite son of Israel.

Joseph has a dream one night. He tells his brothers of his slumbering vision, in which they are all gathering bushels of wheat, and Joseph's bushel stands upright while his brother's bushels bow down to the upright one. This dream intensifies his brothers' hatred for him, for this dream implies that young Joseph will be king over all of his elder brothers - this is not what his brothers want to hear.

Joseph has yet another dream which he shares with his brothers, as well as with Israel. In this dream, the sun, the moon and eleven stars all bow down to Joseph. His father asks Joseph, "What do you mean by this dream of yours?...Are we to come and bow to the ground before you, I and your mother and your brothers?" (37:10) Joseph does not answer his father's question. His brothers grow even more angry and jealous of him.

One day, when Joseph's brothers were out shepherding their father's flocks, Israel calls his favorite son and instructs him to go to his brothers out in the countryside. Joseph puts on his special robe and departs. As he draws near to the field in which they are shepherding, his brothers notice him approaching. "Here comes that dreamer," they say to one another. The brothers plan to kill him, throw his body down into the cistern, and return home to tell their father that a wild beast has devoured him, but God is with Joseph. His brother, Reuben, urges his brothers not to harm Joseph before throwing him into the cistern. Rueben plans on coming back and rescuing his brother later, but he doesn't let his brothers know this.

The brothers seize Joseph when he arrives, strip him of his special robe, and throw him into the empty cistern. After doing this the brothers sit down to eat and notice a caravan of Ishmaelite merchants on their way to Egypt. One of the brothers, Judah, asks the others, "What will be gained by killing our brother? Instead, let us sell him to these merchants." The brothers agree to this, but as this discussion is occurring, passing Midianite merchants draw Joseph up out of the well and sell him to the Ishmaelite caravan for silver. The brothers return to the well to discover that Joseph is gone, so they take the robe, dip it in the blood of a goat they have killed, and return to their father. The brothers show the robe to Israel, and he is convinced that his beloved Joseph has been devoured by a wild beast. Israel is beyond consoling.

Joseph is taken into Egypt and sold to the Pharaoh's captain of the guard, Potiphar. He finds great favor with Potiphar and is put in charge of his vast household and all of his property. One day, Potiphar's wife tries to seduce

Joseph. She takes hold of his loincloth as he runs away and shows it to her husband when he returns home. Potiphar is furious. Potiphar has Joseph thrown into the depths of the prison.

Time passes and two servants of the Pharaoh are imprisoned—the royal cupbearer and the royal baker. One night, these two men experience prolific dreams but are unaware of their deeper meaning, and they become dispirited. Joseph inquires about their worry and finds out that the men desire an interpretation for their dreams. Joseph responds, "All interpretation belongs to God."[14] He listens to the dreams and offers an interpretation to both men that later comes to pass—the cupbearer is restored to his position while the baker is hung. The cupbearer never forgets about Joseph's great gift for interpreting dreams.

More time passes and Pharaoh has two dreams that haunt him to his core. He calls in all of the wise men in Egypt, but not one of them can make any sense of the visions

---

[14] Ibid, 49

that Pharaoh relates. The cupbearer tells Pharaoh of Joseph and his great success in interpreting his dream, as well as the dream of the baker. Pharaoh orders Joseph out of the depths of the prison and into the throne room. There, Joseph hears the dreams in all of their detail. In the first dream, there are seven sleek and fat cows that are devoured by seven gaunt and lean cows, and in the second dream, there are seven ears of corn with full, ripe grains that are swallowed up by seven thin and shriveled ears. Joseph explains that the two dreams are really one.

Joseph interprets that the seven cows and seven ears of a healthy nature represent seven years of bumper harvests, and the seven of each kind of a sickly nature represent seven years of famine. He explains that God is showing to Pharaoh what is going to happen, and Joseph tells Pharaoh to make stock in the years of plenty to survive the years of none. His interpretation comes true, his wisdom is great, and Pharaoh appoints Joseph to a level of power as great as his own. Pharaoh sees that Joseph can clearly hear and listen to God. God is with Joseph, and everything that he influences is truly blessed. Egypt is truly blessed and survives the years of famine.

Individuation, Dreams, Exclusion, & Self-Authority

There are many different archetypes within the story of Joseph that correlate to the process of the nine-year change. From the individuation of the coat, to the interpretation of dreams, to the exclusion of Joseph by his brothers, to the great power obtained in Egypt; the images imply that the child is achieving an individuality, an understanding of Self through feeling, an ability to adapt to the loneliness of ego-consciousness, and an even greater capacity for thinking through feeling. The power of ego-consciousness is beginning to endow the child with the ability to understand the world around her and develop a more authentic and true image of Self.

Individuation

The child has always possessed an individuality of sorts, but so far it has been imitative due to heredity and/or an unconscious response/reaction to the world. The ego-consciousness is the 'middle man' in this process, like a lens standing between inner and outer realities as the eye through which Self and the world are perceived. Like a lens, if it is misshapen or blurry, then the clarity of reality will never be realized without repair or reconstruction. The nine-year change marks a foundational formative shaping of the ego - the beginning of true individuality.

Joseph's new coat with long sleeves covers his trunk and limbs, protecting him from the harshness of the desert environment. Individuality provides the same type of protection for the child, for individuality is the product of a strong ego-consciousness. Just as the coat now holds the body within its fibers, so too is the child being held more and more within their own bodies. They are truly incarnating into their skin and into this world with less reluctance, but with greater intensity. The ego, being drawn into the body, brings consciousness.

As with any new experience, there is a little fear that exists surrounding the unknown, but the more comfortable we become, the less fear inhibits us. Then we are able to delve into the experience with more courage and success. Think about riding a bike—slow and fearful at first with a few falls, but then courage has us going faster with more control. Yet, with greater courage and speed comes the possibility of a more intense fall and serious injury. This is the reality of growth. When we put more on the line, chances are that we can possibly gain more—chances are that we may possibly lose more. Both paths are paths of growth, but there must be a balance.

Interpreting Dreams and Feeling

With a growing courage to hear and settle the Self, the child gains a greater ability for understanding their feelings. This aspect of the changing child is represented by Joseph's ability to recognize and express the dreams that God sends— the ability to understand the feelings pulsing out of the Self. This of course brings the child in close contact with the

Self ,but further away from the world—producing solipsism of feeling.

This solipsism brings understanding, and allows the child to express their feelings to those around them, yet they express these feelings without prior experience, and with little regard for the impact it may have on others. They blurt out with courage, the feelings pulsing within them, without a proactive cognition of the response—much like Joseph. Of course, some children's 'blurting out' can be nonverbal—pure action or withdrawal.

Joseph blurts out his dreams to his family on two different occasions, and these dreams are met with resistance, anger, and jealousy. Unaware of the possible reactions of his family, Joseph shares his dreams without any forethought or 'internal editor'. Joseph has not yet mastered the subtle art of recognizing the potential responses of his audience and tailoring the information in a carefully devised manner.

The child is much the same way, for they are focused deeply inward. The important thing is that the child is expressing the feeling (dreams), for this expression will teach them, after many tough responses, to become less solipsistic and more conscious of others. Through trial and error, the child can come to a sense of compassion for others, and also begin to understand the art of dialogue. We as adults, must allow them to stumble, fail and create woe without stifling the child's courage to express herself—loving firmness is the key.

Exclusion

Now the child is taking their new Self out into the world. This process is unfiltered at first, but the child will eventually learn that we must be conscious of others. Exclusion is a reality that can help to bring the child out of such ego-solipsism. Joseph's unfiltered proclamation of his dreams is the source of his exclusion from his brothers and the land of his family.

His brothers are the lingering ego-consciousness from the downward flow of the stream; they are jealous of Joseph's ability to see the first traces of the light of reemergence—an inner dualistic struggle. Joseph is born to Israel when Israel is in his old age—Joseph is raised and nurtured out of an ego-consciousness that has gained maturity, and inherits the wisdom of the Israel ego. This is the root of his dream interpretation and also his exclusion dreams. This feeling of being cast out is also Joseph's blessing.

The loneliness and exclusion deepens the child's growing sense of individuality and the power associated with it. Exclusion is the process that awakens the child to the interplay between inner and outer realities, to others and their feelings, and to consequences of impulsive actions. The child may experience a feeling of exclusion *without* actually being excluded. This is when your child comes home from school complaining that the other children are leaving her out - they do not let her play. However, when you discuss this with the teacher, they know nothing of this situation and report that the child seems quite happy at school. Even is this is happening to a small degree, this is a positive life experience. Through exclusion, children learn to take into account the feelings of others as they begin to understand that a little forethought, or compassion, can help them avoid harsh reactions. Through this they come to an ever-expanding understanding of their own feelings and sense of Self.

Self-Authority

Joseph finds favor in the land of Egypt. As was mentioned earlier in this book, Egypt is an archetype for the astral, adult world, and Pharaoh represents the authority of the adults in the child's life. Joseph achieves great status in the house of Potiphar, in the prisons of Egypt, and with Pharaoh himself. The child is definitely beginning to emerge into the light-filled vision of the future and leave behind the unconsciousness of childhood. The child is emerging into the beginning of the rest of their lives.

The child's ego-consciousness takes a big step in taming impulsiveness through interpreting their feelings before blurting them outward. Joseph's ability to interpret dreams is the archetype that correlates to this process. Joseph obtains great power because of his ability to interpret dreams and from the blessings that are attached to this new ability. The more accurately the child interprets their feelings, the more power they achieve in the world of adults —the land of Egypt.

The power is respect and recognition of a progressing ego consciousness; they can feel it in our smiles and words of approval. If the dreams of Pharaoh were not interpreted, or clearly interpreted, then Joseph may not have found himself as the right hand man to Pharaoh. But, indeed he did clearly interpret the dreams, and he found favor with Pharaoh in the land of Egypt. Joseph's interpretations of Pharaoh's dreams symbolize the forethought that the child's expanding ego consciousness provides, namely, the realization that we must store up the fruits of our spiritual labors in order to survive the times of spiritual famine.

Joseph becomes a monarch of sorts, as was promised to Abraham's descendants, in the land of Pharaoh. In the apex of the famine, his brothers come to Egypt—the land of bounty. Joseph's earliest dreams come to fruition, and his brothers bow down to him. After a little cunning and forethought on Joseph's part, his whole family joins him in Egypt where he reveals himself, and Joseph forgives his brothers for excluding him and allowing him to be taken out of Canaan. Joseph has now become the monarch of his brothers—as was foreseen in his dreams.

The child too embraces the Joseph ego with all of its abilities and becomes the monarch over the older, immature ego impulses that remain from the downward flow of the stream—represented by his brother's actions, as well as the actions of Potiphar's wife. These lingering ego impulses are like weight that can hinder the upward rising of the stream, so it is not enough to merely lord over them. What is needed is that these older ego impulses must be let go—this is done through forgiveness.

To forgive is to set oneself free from egotism, solipsism, and impulsiveness in order to embrace compassion, community, and interpretation. It is through egotistical Self focus that the child resists the world that is challenging and vast—egotism requires unconsciousness. Therefore, it is through a compassionate Self focus that the child accepts their experiences, desired or undesired, and grows from them through consciousness—the child prepares for a future encounter with the Self much like Moses' encounter with God.

The child is learning to forgive their own impulsiveness, the impulsiveness of others and the world, and even the very 'fall' that has brought them much struggle. The strengthening ego consciousness and an expanded Self awareness are becoming a reality through this struggling. The child is glimpsing the tiny speck of light that awaits them at the point where the stream reemerges. Of course, to the child, this is a strange new force within them and is not experienced as adults experience it. They are by no means masters of the ego, and the child will struggle into the Self for years to come.

The nine year change, at this point, has only been examined two-thirds of the way through its course. The final third is an upward movement that is expressed through the archetypes of Moses. Before we delve into journey of Moses, we must take a look at the quintessential archetype of suffering - Job - in order to truly understand the deep sadness and helplessness that the child may face.

5. JOB, MOSES, AND GOD—A CONCLUSION

"It is at this transition time that the development of the child into an ego-strong or an ego-weak personality is decided."
Rudolf Steiner, Soul Economy and Waldorf Education

"If the children see how adults stand their ground in the face of difficulties of their own destiny, then the spark of ego affirmation grows."
Hermann Koepke, Encountering the Self

The archetypes in the story of Job explain the nature of the child's suffering, occurring during the experience of the nine-year change. Moses has pivotal encounters with God in Exodus—encounters much like the ego has with the Self. We take a look at the relationships between Job and Moses with God, which mirrors the relationship between Self and Ego, while also pointing out the necessity for adult authority.

The story of Job is one of suffering, although he suffers through no fault of his own. He feels overwhelmed, burdened, victimized, and betrayed. This story gives a universal image reflecting the child's own attitude toward her suffering.

Job and the Purpose of Suffering

> *"The story is one of human development. Evil has come into the world. The Fall has taken place. There will be suffering. However it is not suffering for wickedness but one which provides the urge for inner progress. Those on a path of spiritual development suffer trials not of their own making. It is the beginning of the way to God."*
> Roy Wilkinson, *Commentary on the Old Testament Stories*

Job is a blessed man. He has been given nearly everything he has desired. He has money, land, and family. Job is also a righteous man - and why shouldn't he be? God has truly blessed him, and Job praises God for his generosity. In fact, Job is such a righteous man that God holds him up as an example for all to follow. Lucifer goes to God and suggests that the only reason Job is righteous, is because he has been blessed - he bets that if God were to take it all away, that Job would curse his name. So, God puts Job to the test in order to see if he is truly a righteous man.

His servants are killed, his animals stolen, and his family perishes. After a perfect life, he suffers malicious torment at the hands of God and has no idea why. This uncertainty plagues Job as much, if not more than the loss of all his possessions, family, and peace. Job says, "Have I the strength to go on waiting? What end have I to expect, that I should be patient?" (6:11)[15] Job becomes impatient with the endless waves of suffering and seeks to know the reasons behind the undeserved punishment.

The child experiences the nine-year change with the same overall sentiment as Job. Children are plagued with struggles that are not of their own making; rather they are struggles arising from the ego's intense encounters with the Self. These encounters awaken the child to their undeveloped capacity to endure and learn from such consciousness, and this awareness is torture. As Job says, "Oh how shall I find help within myself now that success has been put beyond my reach?" (6:13)[16], and the child has this same struggle, feeling helpless in this new perception—she is

---

[15] Ibid, 515

[16] Ibid, 515

now aware of how much she is *unaware*. Sentience has its own shadow.

Not only does the child feel unequipped, but the tireless anguish is an all-encompassing struggle that makes the experience more intense. As Job says, "God's onslaughts wear me down." (6:4)[17] The Self sends 'floods' of feelings that sweep the child to and fro and overwhelm them to an excess. These floods do flow forth and recede, but to the child they seem perpetual. They may be saying inside themselves: "There is no peace of mind, no quiet for me; trouble comes, and I have no rest." (3:26)[18] When they actually are in a rest period, their peers, who are going through the same experience, will project their struggles outward and keep the onslaughts coming—as if the struggles were singing in perpetual rounds.

Much like Job's peers, the child will find little sympathy or empathy from her classmates, who are just as emotionally unstable and uncertain as the child. They pass

---
[17] Ibid, 515

[18] Ibid, 513

around torment like a flu that won't work its way out of the community—it continues to be recycled. This is important to remember, for it points out that the child has only a few sources for emotional support and stability—parents and teachers. Although the adults must model a strong ego presence, the child will resist this presence, but it still needs to be provided with love and authority.

Job came to mistrust God through his ceaseless anguish, impatience, and inability to understand the reasons behind his misfortune. Job realizes God's inner antinomy, and in the light of this realization, his knowledge attains a divine numinosity.[19] The child tries to make sense of these feelings, just like Job. These feelings test the child just as God tested Job. Children feel like they are being tested by their peers, the world and everyone in it - even themselves. As parents and teachers, we must be the model of faith in the world that has become flawed for the nine-year old child.

---

[19] Jung, Carl *The Portable Jung* (New York: Penguin, 1976), 540

Adults must model a strong Self-authority (ego) for the child to become their own authority—autonomy and individual freedom. The child cannot do this alone; they do not yet possess the tools. We must help them to find these tools, and furthermore, show them how to use them correctly. It is also important to remember that intellectualizing is not what children need! In fact, you can do them harm this way. Instead of definitions and explanations, provide them with kind words with warmth of heart. This period of turbulence can go on for quite some time and it is the warmth from the grown-ups in their lives that will sustain them.

Intellectualizing will not assist the child. When one uses the master carpenter's tools before they are ready, chances are they will cut themselves. Instead of sarcasm and irony, give them empathy. It is through empathy that they will find peace and balance.

In modeling strength of ego, the adult must go beyond personality and subjective reactions that can create more uncertainty in the child's life. We must be stability itself and give the child a feeling of safety through authority and warmth through our unconditional love for them. To avoid intellectualizing will be one of our greatest gifts as parents and teachers, for the child needs adults who they feel have confidence in Self, ego, and their abilities to handle struggle. The child does not think too deeply into why they need to be in the presence of a strong ego; they only need to feel that it is there to be satisfied and fulfilled. The proof for the child is in the feeling experience and not the intellectual experience.

Furnishing "proof" is often taken to be a sign of weakness by the child, for proofs seek to intellectualize something the child experiences as feeling. The child must be allowed to have a true experience of their own. Intellectualizing feelings separates them from us, for they experience their feelings without intellectualizing it. The child needs to be one with feeling before they can begin to cognize it. Until then, children truly live in their soul, and when you experience something within your soul, there is no reason to intellectualize it.

However, children love to test us, and test themselves. Their uncertainty will cause them to ask for proof of all sorts of things; they want to know what we know and how confident we are with our knowledge. Proof is always demanded in cases of uncertainty. If we scurry around trying to prove ourselves, the only thing we prove to the child is that we are uncertain and impulsively seek to verify our knowledge. Parents and teachers, as archetypes, are the only resources the child has to provide certainty in an uncertain world. "Because I say so" is still an appropriate answer for a few more years. When adults try to justify everything to a nine-year old, they are only undermining their own authority.

All of this uncertainty leaves the child in quite a state of turmoil, and they have no idea why! They don't understand that the Self challenges them for the sake of growth. Because she has no awareness of this, the child feels victimized, much like Job. Fortunately, the child will eventually gain more and more success in handling the influx of feelings and fears (shadows) perceived by the ego. Much like Job, "at first he cannot understand the reasons but finally he realizes that they provide a path which leads to the divine."[20] The more they are tested by the Self, the closer they get to it, and the more they are blessed by its offerings of consciousness.

The struggles of the nine-year change are the fertilizer that will help to cultivate ego-consciousness and an understanding of the Self. The development is harsh and requires a seemingly endless string of testing. This is an Exodus of sorts for the child, for there is a promised destination in their future. In order to reach the mountain, the child must make the journey, and, much like the Israelites, there are many struggles along the way.

---

[20] Wilkinson, Roy *Commentaries on the Old testament* (California:Rudolf Steiner College Press, 1993), 36

Moses Sees the Light of Self

> *"Only under a sun without pity,*
> *on a mountain devoid of life,*
> *could the living God break through the cultural filters*
> *that normally protect us from him."*
> Thomas Cahill, *The Gifts of the Jews*

Moses is a symbol of the ego archetype, representing the upward struggle of the stream, back toward the surface, and into the light of consciousness. Moses is a story of a reluctant, uncertain, and humble man who is the medium between God and the world, or rather, his chosen people. The child is a reluctant, uncertain, and, at this point, somewhat humbled human—thanks to Joseph—whose ego-consciousness is the medium between Self and the world.

The Burning Bush

> *"The self...is a God-image"*
> Carl Jung, *The Portable Jung*

Moses' encounters with God were different from the patriarchal fathers, for they only heard a disembodied voice. Moses, however, not only heard the voice, but he also beheld the burning light of God, within a bush, high atop a mountain. In relation to the stream, the light of the world above is now seen, and the dialogue between ego and the Self becomes evermore personal, up close, and powerful. It is like having a relationship via phone, internet, etc. and then one day the person is met for the first time face to face. Their reality and existence expand exponentially within our consciousness and the person takes on a whole new dimension within our perceptual reality. The Moses ego has such an experience with God.

When Moses noticed a burning bush upon the mountain Sinai, he turned to it with curiosity, wonder, and an inner impulse. God wanted Moses to see him; he wanted to make his presence known in a new and powerful way.

> When the Lord saw that Moses had turned aside to look, he called to him out of the bush, 'Moses, Moses!' He answered, 'Here I am!' God said...'I am the God of your father, the God of Abraham, Isaac, and Jacob.' (3:4-6)[21]

---

[21]Oxford University *Oxford Study Bible* (New York:Oxford University Press, 1992), 64

It would be like the Self calling to the ego, "Ego, Ego! I am the Self of all your evolving ego incarnations thus far." Seeing the Self for the first time, in the light of consciousness, is an experience that is as exciting as it is frightening.

Moses is a little apprehensive when God tells him that he is the one who shall lead the Israelites out of the land of Egypt and out of the slavery of Pharaoh.

> 'But who am I', Moses said to God, 'that I should approach Pharaoh and that I should bring the Israelites out of Egypt?' God answered, 'I am with you.' (3:11-12)[22]

Moses knows that he will be taking on Pharaoh and his ruling authority and power. He is uncertain about his abilities and whether the power of this God will match up against the earthly power of Egypt. But now he knows that God is with him.

The child, in a sense, is also seeking to free itself from the bondage of authority. Even though we must never stop modeling, it is time to let them go have their own

---

[22] Ibid

experiences and make their own mistakes, for this is the only path to knowledge. They will continually command us, verbally or non-verbally, as Moses said to Pharaoh, "Let my people go!" The child seeks Self-authority by breaking away from the rule of parents (Egypt). Individuation depends upon this struggle and assertion of Self.

The Self beckons the child to strengthen her ego-consciousness so that it may be the Self authority that is the mediator between inner and outer worlds. The ego must become the 'monarch' of the wandering and expanding consciousness of the child. Like Moses, the child feels that the Self is the voice that has been leading them into the world for a long time—it is who they are. The child comes to feel that the Self will be with them forever, but they must question the Self like Moses questioned God when he asked for his name. "God answered, 'I Am that I am...This is my name for ever; this is my title in every generation." (3:14-15)[23] The light of Self has been seen and

---

[23] Ibid

the child finally just begins to feel that they are the Self. In so many ways they proclaim to the world, "I am this Self; this Self am I!" Dr. Suess was on to something with the opening lines of *Green Eggs and Ham* — "I am Sam. Sam I am."

The Commandments

> "With regard to the Ten Commandments, these are mostly negatives giving clear guidance as to what should not be done.
> The Israelites were not yet sufficiently mature to decide for themselves. The ego forces were not yet fully awake."
> Roy Wilkinson, *Commentaries on the Old Testament*

In order to make it to the Promised Land, the child must live by the rules of the Self—as Moses and his people must live by the rules of God. Otherwise, the suffering and duration of their trek will only intensify and increase. The giving of the Ten Commandments represents this need for structure in order to achieve Self-authority in guiding the ego towards strength. Moses needed the strength of the commandments to guide his people, and the child needs them too.

The Self gives commandments to the child, but the child is not able to translate them. God gives the commandments to Moses, written by the hand of the Spirit, but Moses cannot read them. Moses goes back to the mountain and this time, takes a dictation from God. While the first set of commandments were written by God own hand, this time, they are taken down by Moses. The child, like Moses, must rewrite these inner rules in their own language with their own hand.

It has been mentioned many times now that children need example in which to follow. Assuming this has been done, the child can now begin to write their own inner commandments. However, we must be careful not to impose our own personal rules upon their tablets, but we can model how we come to our own Self commandments. As parents and teachers, we can share the universal commandments of the world that are archetypal to humanity—the experiences and 'rules' that speak to each human soul without the need for proof. This will only shine through to the child if we can be the unquestioned (although constantly questioned) authority within their lives.

> For you cannot work with children of this age, as their teacher, unless you yourself are the unquestioned authority, unless, that is, the children have the feeling: this is true because you hold it to be true, this is beautiful because you find it beautiful, and this is good because you think it good—and therefore you are pointing these things out. You must be for the children the representative of the good, the true, and the beautiful. The children must be drawn to truth, goodness, and beauty simply because the children are drawn to you yourself.[24]

Children require an example of how a human being has come to recognize the truths, beauties, and goodness of the world.

Children will retain their belief in your authority, and that is good for the child's further education, but it is also essential that just at the age between nine and ten the child's belief in a good person is strong. The child needs to see where they are going; why they struggle and the rewards that can be reaped from such hard work.

---

[24] Steiner, Rudolf *The Kingdom of Childhood* (New York: Anthroposophical Press, 1995), 34

The Stream Emerges

Now that the child has wandered through the desert, made her own way, written her rules, and found her inner voice, she can begin to make sense of this new world. She no longer remains within the shadows as the stream of change finally comes back out into the light. While there may still be some lingering sadness or anger, things as a whole, seem much brighter now, and our children are much easier to live with. Finally!

While this is essentially a journey that children complete on their own, in their own time, it is our duty as teachers and parents to be aware and conscious of the child's development so that we may honor and guide the child in the proper way. If we put the harsh fertilizers of intellectualism upon their sprouting ego, we may burn the fragile infant growth that is just beginning to reach out towards the light. But, if we recognize the stage of the child's growth, then we will know that a gentler fertilizer of loving authority will provide the sprouting ego-consciousness with what it shall need to grow into strong stems. As Rudolf Steiner wrote:

> It is of [great] importance to know what happens at a certain point in a child's life and how you should act with regard to it, so that through your action you may radiate light onto the child's whole life.[25]

The rest of the child's life depends upon their first conscious judgment, observations, and realizations of the world, the Self, and the ego that perceives both. I hope that this book has served as a conceptual "road map", or "stream map", to the nine and ten year old child, and their experience through this pivotal life moment known as *the nine-year change.*

---

[25] Ibid, 34

Bibliography

Cahill, Thomas. *The gifts of the Jews.* New York, NY: Anchor Books. 1998

Dunne, John S. *Time and myth.* New York, NY: University of Notre Dame Press/Doubleday. 1975

Edmunds, Francis. *Rudolf Steiner education.* London, England: Rudolf Steiner Press. 1986

Harwood, A. C. *The recovery of man in childhood.* New York, NY: The Myrin Institute. 1958

Hegel, G. W. F. *Reason in history.* Englewood Cliffs, NJ: Prentice-Hall Inc. 1953

Johnson Fenner, P. & K. L. Rivers. *Waldorf education.* Amesbury, MA: Michaelmus Press. 1995

Jung, Carl. *The portable Jung.* New York, NY: Penguin Books. 1976

Koepke, Hermann. *Encountering the self.* Hudson, NY: Anthroposophical Press. 1989

Oxford University. *Oxford study bible.* New York, NY: Oxford University Press. 1992

Pascal Ph.L., Eugene. *Jung to live by.* New York, NY: Warner Books. 1992

Spock, Marjorie. *The lively art of teaching.* Hudson, NY: Anthroposophical Press. 1985

Steiner, Rudolf. *Ancient myths & the new Isis mystery.* Hudson, NY: Anthroposophical Press. 1994

Steiner, Rudolf. *The child's changing consciousness.* New York, NY: Anthroposophical Press. 1998

Steiner, Rudolf. *The kingdom of childhood.* Hudson, NY: Anthroposophical Press. 1995

Wilkinson, Roy. *Commentaries on the Old Testament.* Sacramento, CA: Rudolf Steiner College Press. 1993

Wilkinson, Roy. *Old Testament stories.* Sussex, England: Forrest Row. 1985

Made in United States
North Haven, CT
05 July 2023